MW01063455

Secrets of a Dog Trainer

Secrets of a Dog Trainer

Victoria Schade

WILEY

Turner Publishing Company/Howell Book House
424 Church Street • Suite 2240 • Nashville, Tennessee 37219
445 Park Avenue • 9th Floor • New York, New York 10022

www.turnerpublishing.com

SECRETS OF A DOG TRAINER: POSITIVE PROBLEM SOLVING FOR A WELL-BEHAVED DOG

Library of Congress Cataloging-in-Publication Data

Schade, Victoria.
Secrets of a dog trainer : positive problem solving for a well-behaved dog / Victoria Schade.
pages cm
Includes index.
ISBN 978-1-118-50929-6
1. Dogs--Training. 2. Dogs--Behavior. I. Title.
SF431.S333 2014
636.7'0835--dc23

2014016153

Printed in the United States of America
14 15 16 17 18 19 0 9 8 7 6 5 4 3 2 1

For Tom, my favorite person.

CONTENTS

Secrets of a Dog Trainer

INTRODUCTION: LIFE WITH OLIVE

"Don't you know who *am?*" I asked our new puppy, Olive, as I attempted to wipe her paws, only half joking.

Olive had let out an unmistakable growl at me for toweling her feet after our millionth (and now rainy) potty-training trip to the yard. I was shocked. My shiny new ten-week-old puppy had handling issues? I was so caught off guard that I found myself saying, "Hey! Knock it off, Olive!"

Whoops.

I regretted saying it the second the words were out of my mouth, as I knew they would do nothing to solve the problem percolating at my feet. I was embarrassed by my reaction and how I had responded to the growl without thinking. I recovered from my surprise and snapped back into dog-trainer mode, ready to address her reactivity the right way.

Clearly my new puppy had no clue that she was living under the same roof as a dog trainer who had built her career working with puppies. (My initial reaction to her growl certainly didn't clue her in!) All she knew was

Is this the face of a puppy with body-handling issues? This photo was taken right around the time when Olive growled at me when I tried to wipe her paws.

that what I was doing to her paws didn't feel right, and she wanted to let me know that I needed to stop it. So I did.

As I addressed Olive's handling issue the proper way—more on the specifics later—I pondered how her behavior could develop if I continued telling her to "stop it" when she growled at me. My initial response was visceral and without thought, which is a dicey approach to dog training. I was lucky in that I had the tools to deal with her reactivity, but I considered what could happen in the average non-dog-trainer household, where telling a growly puppy to "quit it" is probably a knee-jerk reaction. Unfortunately, knee-jerk reactions to dog problems are rarely the *right* reactions.

It's helpful to have *mindful interactions* with our dogs—to think about why we're doing what we're doing, and what impact it will have on our dogs' behavior—particularly when they're young and impressionable. Forcing ourselves to be aware of how we work with our dogs, and to realize that every interaction is a potential lesson, can prevent missteps like the one I went through with Olive on that rainy evening. Even though I live and breathe the concept of mindful interactions with my clients, it was easy to fall prey to a quick response that could have damaged the bond with my growing puppy.

Scolding a puppy for growling is a common mistake that doesn't seem like a big deal, but how could my admonition have affected Olive's long-term behavior if I had kept it up? Let's explore three potential outcomes.

Scenario One: Frustrated by Olive's "dominance" growling, I escalate to yelling at her and wrestling with her each time I need to wipe off her paws. I don't let go or loosen my grip when she growls; I simply holler louder and grab on tighter. She responds by growling more ferociously and showing her teeth, and I often worry that she might bite me. It's an unpleasant task for both of us, but necessary, as her feathered paw fur collects a lot of mud. On rainy days I'm forced to trap her before she comes in the house in order to clean her paws. It's a frustrating, messy dance. When she manages to slip by me, I wind up chasing her through the house, maddened by the muddy paw prints she leaves everywhere. I'm really upset by the time I catch her, and she's stressed out.

Scenario Two: Olive and I struggle mightily at paw-wiping time, and her discomfort with my handling leaks into other areas, like tooth brushing and nail trimming. Because she already dislikes having her feet handled, cutting her nails is nearly impossible. She runs when she sees the clippers come out, and when I manage to corner her, she growls and bites at the clipper. I'm nervous to continue clipping her nails on my own, so I ask my veterinarian to do it. Olive has never liked going to her vet, which is no surprise given her aversion to *my* handling, let alone a stranger with a thermometer. She's been "mouthy" during exams in the past—she has a yellow sticker on her file that suggests the need for careful handling—so the veterinarian gingerly

On Dominance

In the old-school training world, it seems that anything a dog does that humans don't agree with can be chalked up to "dominance." Jumping up, urine marking, pulling on the leash, growling—these behaviors are quite natural in the dog world, but somehow they morph into power struggles in our households according to trainers who believe in a "pack theory" behavioral hierarchy. Viewing these types of behaviors through the prism of dominance allows for indignation to creep in, as in, "How *dare* you challenge me, dog?" Decisions made with this attitude can cause long-term problems rather than provide solutions. When you consider that the dog that urine-marks in the house might not be fully housetrained, or the dog that growls when you try to trim his nails might have had a painful nail trim in the past, you can approach the problem from a more accepting dog-friendly perspective.

attempts the first paw. Olive growls and bites him hard enough that her teeth leave indentations on his skin, so he calls for assistance and a muzzle. Putting on the muzzle requires an extra set of hands, as Olive bucks and gnashes so wildly that she nearly falls off the table. One vet tech holds her body and one stabilizes her head as the veterinarian slips the muzzle over her mouth. Olive is trembling with fear, but she still jerks her head toward the veterinarian's hand each time the clipper cuts through a nail. I stand by, sad for my dog and embarrassed at what I've just witnessed.

Scenario Three: Olive growls at me when I wipe her paws, and I yell loudly enough to frighten her and suppress the growling. Even though she no longer growls when I towel off her feet, she cowers when I do it and keeps her body very stiff. She tucks her tail between her legs, ducks her head as I reach for her, and leans away from me as I work. She still tries to escape as I wipe her down, but I can tell it's because she's afraid of me and what I'm doing to her. Sometimes when I reach out to pet her, she moves away from me. My young niece visits on a rainy weekend, and I ask her to wipe Olive's paws before they come in from the yard. She attempts to do it, and Olive growls and quickly nips her hand before she even touches the rag to her paw.

Now, the three scenarios presented above are *possible* scenarios, not guaranteed outcomes. Olive could very well have continued her low-level growling at me without taking it to the next level, but that's not a chance I was willing to take. I wanted Olive to welcome, or, at the very least, graciously tolerate, typical health-and-wellness routines, and the only way to make that happen was to address her growly reaction head-on. Letting a problem fester instead of actively working on it allows the behavior to take root in a dog's behavioral repertoire. I was unwilling to live with an unhappy, growly dog during the rain and mud season, and I didn't relish the thought of potential "spin-off" behavioral problems that could sprout from her handling issues.

Often, major canine challenges stem from humble beginnings. The tiny puppy that pulls on his leash when he walks can become the uncontrollable sled dog when he matures. The dog who gets a laugh every time he barks at the doorbell can become the nonstop alarm barker that drives his family crazy. The adolescent rescue dog that still puts her teeth on skin when she plays tug might become the dog that nips a neighbor child during a rough-and-tumble game of fetch. We don't always think ahead as to how a seemingly "throw-away" behavior can morph into something much more troubling. Engaging in mindful interactions with your dog will allow you to take a step back and ask yourself, "If I interact with my dog in this way, is his response a behavior that I can live with?" Taking a moment to evaluate your interactions with your dog might well prevent problems from developing.

So how did I prevent the potential scenarios regarding the paw-wiping issue from becoming a reality?

Rather than continue to try to suppress Olive's growling by yelling at her, I acknowledged that she was uncomfortable with what I was doing, and I backed off. Now, this wasn't a case of me letting her assert her "dominance" over me. (An outdated school of thought suggests never letting your dog "win" in a confrontation, as once she does she thinks that she is the "alpha" in the household. That's old-fashioned thinking that behavioral science has debunked in myriad ways.) Instead of allowing Olive to practice and perfect growling when I wiped her paws, I wanted to teach her to *accept* what she considered aversive handling. An easy way to do this is with "touch for a treat."

I picked a time to work on training when I knew I didn't need to wipe Olive's paws, as it's best for the dog to practice appropriate reactions frequently before the final exam—that is, when you actually need to use the behavior in real life. Rather than pick up Olive's paw as I had done when she growled at me, I started with an *approximation* of the finished behavior, or a highly stylized version of what a paw wipe would actually look and feel like. This allowed her gradually to become comfortable with the process without feeling the need to react.

I took the rag, gently tapped it on the top of Olive's paw quickly, and handed over a treat. Olive's reaction seemed to say, "Hey, that wasn't bad at all!" so I attempted another gentle tap on the same foot. Touch, and then treat. This not-so-aversive touch predicts a very desirable treat, so in time, Olive would begin to accept the wipe-down.

I kept the treats out of sight on a high counter while we practiced. Olive is incredibly food driven (I'd call her "food mad"), and I wanted to ensure that she was able to focus on what I was doing with her feet and not the treat hovering just a few inches away. Keeping the treat visible during the "touch-for-a-treat" training could turn it into a bribe, or a way of saying, "If you let me touch your foot, you'll get this goody." While bribery is not a *completely* negative option in a training scenario like this one, I knew that I wanted to eventually wean Olive off needing a treat for each paw wipe—I didn't want to be captive to the food for life. (Plus it's tough to wipe paws while holding a treat at the same time!) To keep the entire procedure fumble-free, I took the treats out of the bag to avoid the telltale crinkly noise.

Because dogs are good at picking up on rhythms and patterns, I tried to make my touches unpredictable. The first few touches for a treat were quick, and then I touched the top of her foot and held the rag there for a one-two count, followed by the treat. The final paw touch of the session was another quick one, followed by the treat and lots of praise. Though her initial "touch-for-a-treat" training went beautifully and would have been easy to keep going, I knew that it was best to leave her wanting more.

I continued the training over the next few days, keeping the sessions short and fun. After tapping the rag lightly on the top of all of her paws with varying degrees of pressure and duration and then delivering the treat, I started to actually pick up her paws and quickly swipe the rag across them. Again, I varied the way I grasped her paw in my hand, as well as the pressure I used when I wiped. My goal as I worked through this process was to ensure that I never pushed Olive so that she felt the need to react. I never wanted to elicit that growly reaction again! I needed her to remain calm and comfortable as I touched her so that she would come to realize that my hands bring good things, even when dealing with a dicey body part like her feet.

The next time the rains hit, we were ready. She came inside and willingly sat on the carpet square by the door when she saw me standing by with the rag. (At this point the rag predicted good stuff!) I asked her, "May I wipe?" a silly formality that had become a part of our process, and got to work. She watched me intently as I rubbed her paws, because my "real-world" wiping probably felt different from our practice rounds. (I didn't realize just how muddy those little paws could get!) I praised her the entire time, pleased that we had worked through this challenge as a team. What made me even happier was that she generalized my foot-handling training to other scenarios. During her first few baths, she growled when I scrubbed near her tail and back feet. I did a single session with treats during a bath, and from that point on she tolerated the handling like a trooper. Her reaction to my handling went from "I really don't like what you're doing so *stop it,*" to "This isn't my favorite thing to do with you, but I can deal with it." She became so comfortable with my handling that nail trims became a breeze as well! (She actually lifts each paw to offer it to me, a move that melts my heart.)

Not all behavioral problems work out this quickly. I was lucky on a few counts: Olive had just started growling, so the behavior wasn't entrenched in her repertoire yet; paw wiping wasn't something I had to deal with every day so I could take my time addressing it; and, well, I'd had some experience with the whole "touch for a treat" training process over the years!

It's best to address a problem before it takes root, of course, but that's not always possible. Sometimes it's not easy to see a budding problem for what it could become. A puppy's jumpy greeting starts off as an adorable way to say hello but becomes a literal pain when the dog hits full size. By then, after the dog has had months of practice, the jumping is entrenched, and it's also highly rewarding for the dog. Mindful interactions require us to see beyond the immediate behavior before us and envision how life will be if the behavior continues on its current course.

A customer of mine, Dana, recently brought her new puppy, Loki, into the small dog shop I own. The poor pup had been out and about all day, so she could barely stay awake for the introduction. We were both in awe of the tiny, sleepy lab. Knowing what I know about labs, I took the opportunity to preach to Dana while the pup napped at our feet.

"Dana, you have a clean-slate dog. She's just nine weeks old; this is your chance to do everything right! You can teach Loki the proper way to greet people so that she never jumps up, and you can teach her how to walk politely without pulling. You can teach her to be the *perfect dog!*" I became a little wild-eyed and unhinged as I tried to express to Dana how important it was to begin training immediately.

"Oh, we're going to start working on "sit" and "down" right away," Dana replied.

"That's great, but I'm talking about all the little stuff that happens between you guys every day. The jumping, for example. When people pet her, does she jump up on them?"

"Um, I haven't noticed it yet . . ."

"Great!" I interrupted her. "Keep it that way!"

I went on to explain quickly to Dana how she could prevent typical bad habits like jumpy greetings and leash pulling from developing, and she seemed to take in what I was saying. We parted ways, and I wished her luck with Loki.

Cut to three months later and a frustrated Dana back in my store.

"Loki is so bad! She runs away, she's awful on the leash, she jumps on everyone and everything . . ."

Can you imagine how disappointed I was? Granted, Loki was still a very young dog, but now Dana would have to focus on changing unpleasant behaviors that could have been prevented in the first place. Had Dana stopped to think about her interactions with Loki—those mindful interactions again—she could have asked herself, "Do I like this behavior? Do I want it to continue?" Dogs do what "works" for them, meaning they do what is rewarding to them in some way. So if jumping and leash pulling bring Loki some sort of satisfaction, whether her person's attention or getting to go where she wants to go, she will continue to perform the behaviors.

We all don't have the same "clean-slate" luxury afforded to Dana and young Loki. Adult rescue dogs might arrive in their new homes with well-rehearsed behavioral challenges, like leash pulling or barking, that their new guardians discover post-adoption. The behaviors have taken root, so is it too late? The good news is that it's never too late to begin working on behavioral challenges. The speed of resolution, however, depends on factors like the age of onset (did the dog start guarding her food bowl as a puppy or as an adult when a new dog was added to the household?), how long the dog has performed the behavior (a well-practiced behavior can take longer to resolve), the severity of the issue (does the "biting dog" leave a only a coating of saliva on the skin when he bites, or does he break skin?), and most important, how dedicated the guardian is to working through the problem. I wish that I could say that every fix is easy, but that's just not the case.

This book covers a wide array of canine challenges, from problems that we all could potentially face during our dog's lifetime to those that are more specialized. The book addresses these problems in two ways: it serves as a cautionary tale to *prevent* problems from developing, and it offers solutions to those already in the throes of a canine challenge. Each problem is illustrated by a case study that describes the situation, followed by several "choose-your-own-ending" outcomes that explain what might happen if the problem continues unchecked. It's important to note that the outcomes are not guarantees, nor are they the *only* outcomes that could occur.

I am an unapologetic treat trainer. Nearly all of the behavior problems described in this book are addressed using food as a reward. Unfortunately, there are still many holdouts regarding training using treats. People say that they want their dog to "work for me" and not resort to bribery, and that a dog's "natural instinct to please her master" should be enough to encourage appropriate responses. Typically these people use outdated compulsion-type training with choke chains and corrections. So even if the old-school trainer believes that the dog is "working for him" while using a choke collar, the dog is actually working to avoid a painful correction from the collar. People need to understand that training with treats is not bribery. Bribery is showing the dog the food in your hand and saying, "Will you sit now?" Reward training is asking the dog to sit, and then following up with the treat as a reward for a job well done. People worry that treat training enslaves you to dishing out food forever. Done properly, however, training with food should allow for the treats to be weaned over time until your dog only gets the occasional intermittent reward. My dogs perform a myriad of

Before You Begin Problem Solving

1. Identify the exact problem: Use a clinician's perspective when identifying a problem, and take emotion out of the equation. Don't say, "My dog rips up all of my stuff because she's mad at me for going back to work." Be specific and factual, as in, "My dog steals my shoes and chews on them." Then get even more specific. "My dog steals my shoes and chews on them when he hasn't gotten enough exercise."
2. Identify any ancillary issues related to the problem: Perhaps the shoe stealing happens only when your dog is in the house alone? Or perhaps your dog is going through a chewing phase and doesn't have enough appropriate outlets for chewing?
3. Admit your possible role in the problem: Of course, the dog guardian isn't always involved in the development of a behavioral problem, but truth be told, sometimes we accidentally create our own monsters. Did you give your puppy old flip flops to chew on? Did you forget to puppy-proof? Is your dog getting the exercise she needs? Admitting your participation in the behavioral problem takes some of the pressure off your dog and might make you more aware of how your actions affect your dog's behavior.

behaviors without needing treats, like polite leash walking, paw wiping, and cute tricks like "sit pretty" and "roll over."

I also believe in rewarding with play, like fetch and tug, although sometimes play as a reward can be cumbersome as compared to tossing a biscuit to your dog. Whatever your dog decides is her most powerful reinforcer, whether play or food, using "intermittent reinforcement" to dole out that reward is one of the most effective ways to keep a behavior alive.

When it comes to problem behaviors, it seems that everyone, from your veterinarian to the person who does your taxes, has an opinion about the best way to solve dog problems. There are widely divergent opinions in the dog-training community as well, with advice coming from those who still believe in old-school models of pack theory and dominance, to those who have continued to educate themselves on the latest findings in canine behavioral science. *My* advice regarding advice is to always do a gut check before you carry through with it. Even if the suggestion comes from the veterinarian your family has used for twenty years, if it doesn't feel right for you and your dog, don't do it. Avoid doing anything where you feel as though you're physically hurting your dog, or damaging your relationship with her. There is a always a positive, dog-friendly way to work through every canine challenge, and this book will help you do just that.

part one

PUPPY PROBLEMS

In my experience, puppyhood brings in two unique but related stages. Stage one is the "proud-parent" period, when you're floored by the ridiculously cute new family member in your home. *Everything* your puppy does is adorable! When you take your puppy out in public, he literally stops traffic. You can't believe your good fortune that this fluffy ball of sweetness is your new best friend. You've got a serious case of puppy fever.

Stage two is the "awakening" period. It's the moment when you realize that your new best friend is a helluva lot of work. Potty training is all-consuming and more difficult than you'd imagined. The puppy's energy level is jaw dropping—you just want to sit and watch some TV, but your pup has other ideas. Your kids have holes in their T-shirts and scratches on their arms, and they're a little afraid of the puppy. The "creature" is taking over your house, you're living in a maze of baby gates, and you're feeling ambivalent about your decision to bring home a dog. You doubt your sanity and quietly wish for your old life pre-puppy.

You're not alone. Nearly everyone has a moment—or in some cases, weeks worth of "moments"—in which they wish they had never gotten a puppy. I hate to admit it, but I did. Olive brought chaos into our orderly lives, and even though I had the tools to deal with anything she threw my way, we had a very, very challenging few months. From her refusal to take to the crate to her general "disconnectedness" (which is a politically correct way of saying I think that my dog has special needs), Olive proved to be unlike any other dog I've ever known, and so I often doubted my decision.

Because life with Olive was so challenging, I worked doubly hard to keep burgeoning problems like her growling from taking root. The growling at such a young age didn't sound like a threat—it was sort of silly to hear such a tiny dog asserting herself! The fact is, many typical dog problems have adorable beginnings in puppyhood. When the pup jumps up for attention, we lean down and pet it. Nipping is encouraged through rough play. And those tiny tough-guy "yip yips" when the doorbell chimes are hysterical! We allow puppies to get away with behaviors we wouldn't tolerate in adult dogs because they seem harmless, but by allowing them and often accidentally encouraging them, we're setting the stage for the behavior to continue. Unfortunately, dogs don't grow out of behaviors like jumping, nipping, and barking. Once again, the idea of mindful interactions with our dogs comes into play. In puppyhood it helps to repeat the mantra: Do I like the behavior? Do I want to see it continue?

There's an old dog-training truism that says, "You get the dog you deserve." That expression can be interpreted a couple of ways: the dog that you "craft" through every interaction is the dog you deserve, meaning you raise the dog so that he is a product of all that you teach him. The other meaning is that the dog you end up with was "sent" to you to teach you a lesson. Obviously, the first interpretation makes the most sense, but I like to get metaphysical and take the second one into account as well. The dogs I've been "sent" over the years have taught me many timely lessons. Sumner, our wonderful Boxer that was featured in my last book, *Bonding with Your Dog: A Trainer's Secrets for Building a Better Relationship,* came to us at a year old with severe socialization and leash-reactivity issues. I was in the infancy of my dog-training career when we adopted him, and he taught me so much about dealing with challenging (and embarrassing) leash issues. I was able to translate the scientific approach toward counterconditioning and desensitization to one that could work in the real world. (Life doesn't happen in a laboratory, and even the most effective training plans can be tough to work out on the streets.) Sumner was my greatest training project. He went from hating the sight of other dogs to mellowing out enough to be a shop dog in my little dog store. He was living, breathing proof that dog-friendly dog training works, even for those dogs that seem hopeless.

Olive came to me at a time when I'd grown overconfident about my puppy-training skills. I was convinced that I'd have her housetrained within two weeks, and that she'd be a textbook-perfect student in all things training. I was in for a rude awakening. Olive had challenges that I couldn't even begin to understand or explain, even though we adopted her at a youthful eight weeks old. It took me only a few days to realize that she didn't seem . . . normal. Potty training her took *months,* not weeks, and not because I was lax. She exhibited a series of disconnects that I couldn't understand, and I wondered if her airway had been cut off during the birthing process. (I'm not making light—she's *truly* odd in a thousand different ways.) I would never call her stupid, though. She's actually cunning at times, but she also can't figure out how to get off the porch if she can't see the steps right in front of her. Olive proved to me that even the most diligent of dog guardians can be faced with challenges beyond their control or understanding. She gave me empathy for everyone who stumbles through training, content to celebrate baby steps.

one

CRATE TRAINING

Crate training is an often misunderstood part of a dog's growing up. To us it seems cruel to lock a puppy up in a wire box, but the crate taps into a dog's natural desire to den, plus it keeps your dog safe and dry when you can't watch him. A properly sized crate that is introduced with care will become your puppy's comfortable second home.

The crate is a training tool that can get retired after a dog is reliably potty and chew trained. Many dogs learn to love their crates, however, and prefer to sleep in them for years. I've always considered it a means to an end, though, and I like transitioning my dogs from their crates to comfy beds placed throughout the house. That said, during the initial phases of potty training, the crate should be a best friend to both you *and* your puppy!

Case Study: Jane brought home her eight-week-old Rottweiler puppy after doing a great deal of research on responsible breeders. She felt confident and ready to do everything right with her new pup. She had prepped her house and purchased two wire crates; one was set up in the family room and the other in her bedroom. Jane understood why the crate was important and was ready to use it, but what she hadn't anticipated was her deep and immediate attachment to her new puppy. The first time she placed Beamer in the crate, the pup whimpered and paced the length of the giant crate, so she took him out right away and comforted him. She felt *terrible* about putting her baby in it! She tried again that evening, and even though Beamer was exhausted from his first day home, he woke up right away and whimpered again. The cries weren't panicked, just those of typical puppy displeasure. To Jane he sounded pathetic. She was sure that he was missing his mom and siblings, so she placed the groggy dog next to her on the couch, where he proceeded to fall into a snoring slumber. Jane placed her hand on Beamer's warm little body and decided that she would get serious about crate training in the morning.

Despite Jane's good intentions, the pattern continued. She'd place Beamer in the crate and then become immediately distraught when her puppy vocalized. She tried to let him "cry it out" several times, but after four or five minutes of yelping with no end in sight, Jane would open the crate and comfort Beamer. When she went to work, she would leave Beamer in the gated-off kitchen, with the wire crate open and available to him. Beamer never opted to use the crate. Instead, when Jane came home at the end of the day, she would often find Beamer curled up in the corner near the refrigerator. She also found puddles and piles scattered throughout the kitchen, despite the fact that she had hired a dog walker to take Beamer out while she was at work.

Eventually the crate became just another piece of furniture. She kept the door closed and stacked her laundry on top of the crate in her bedroom but held out the hope that Beamer might decide to use the one in the kitchen. The door to that crate was always open, but never used.

Possible Outcome One: Because Beamer never learned to accept the crate, he had free rein of the kitchen and family room. Jane knew that she was supposed to keep her puppy in sight at all times when he was loose, as he was essentially a baby without a diaper, and she *tried* to keep an eye on him. Watching Beamer seemed easy in theory—until she received an important phone call that required her undivided attention, or when she got wrapped up in her favorite reality program. Beamer walked on whisper-quiet paws, so it was difficult to notice when the puppy made his way out of the room and to his favorite indoor potty spot. He had daily accidents of both varieties. At four months old, his puddles and piles were becoming more substantial, but Jane didn't know how to curtail them. She took him outside consistently and rewarded him for pottying outside, but the indoor accidents didn't stop. They lessened over time thanks to Jane's dedication to taking Beamer out frequently, but he continued to have at least one indoor accident a week until he was almost eight months old.

Possible Outcome Two: Jane often spent time on the computer when she was home in the evening. She allowed ten-week-old Beamer to rest near her feet beneath the desk, all the while breathing a sigh of relief that her active puppy was settled quietly instead of running through the house. One evening, after a particularly intense research session online, Jane leaned down to give her resting puppy a belly rub. She was surprised to find Beamer wide awake. He had been so quiet and still that Jane was sure he had fallen asleep. She took a closer look and discovered something black under his paw. A pen cap, perhaps? Jane reached for the contraband and was shocked to see that her puppy had managed to chew his way through the cord to her brand-new printer! One end remained plugged into the wall, and the other dangled limply in her hand. Jane was relieved that the expensive printer was turned off but horrified to think that her puppy could have injured himself while sitting so close to her.

It doesn't have to be scary! The crate should be a place of respite and comfort for your puppy.

Now let's hit the rewind button. How should Jane have addressed Beamer's initial reticence to be crated?

Pick the Correct Crate Size

Jane selected Beamer's crates with his end weight in mind, which potentially could have been up to 100 pounds. When Beamer came home at eight weeks, he was just eleven pounds, so he had way too much room to wander in his giant crate. A crate's size should allow for the puppy to stand comfortably and to turn around and lie down, but not much bigger. Because most puppies from healthy environments have an innate desire to keep their sleeping area clean (although puppies that come from pet stores in which they spend all of their time crated have probably lost this inclination), the narrow confines of a properly sized crate prevent them from soiling one area and resting safe and clean in a far corner. Had Jane kept Beamer in the too-big crate, it's likely that he would have done just that.

There are two primary types of crates: airline crates and wire crates. As the name suggests, airline crates are the type that are accepted in the cargo section of planes. The typical airline crate is usually made of hard plastic, either with small wire inserts along the top or holes in the plastic for air flow, along with a wire door. Wire crates are made of heavy-duty steel wire with a plastic pan liner at the bottom, and resemble a cage. In my experience, dogs don't take to airline crates as readily as the wire type. My guess is that the restricted sightlines in an airline crate make the dog feel too confined. While crates are *supposed* to be denlike, my anecdotal evidence suggests that there is such a thing as being too "denned in."

For puppies that will go through exponential growth, like Beamer, you can either purchase a large crate that will accommodate the dog at its full-grown size, or a smaller "puppy crate" as well as a bigger crate when the pup grows out of the small one. If you opt to purchase the largest-size crate your dog will need, make sure to pick up a crate divider as well. This metal partition reduces the available space in a crate and can be moved to accommodate the puppy as he grows.

Select the Right Bedding

It's tempting to put the biggest, fluffiest bed in the crate for your puppy. You want your baby to be comfortable in there, right? The problem with over-stuffed bedding is that if your puppy has an accident, it might get absorbed and therefore make it difficult to tell that it happened. In addition, big puffy beds can become a tempting distraction for the bored puppy and just get chewed up.

Opt for thin bedding instead, like an old beach towel, that your puppy will be less likely to destroy. If your puppy can't resist even the most boring of liners, it's okay to remove it for a few weeks until your pup has matured enough to refrain from chewing it.

Acclimate the Puppy to the Crate Slowly

Though it *is* difficult to hear a young puppy whining in the crate, sometimes it's a necessary step in the process. Giving the puppy time to explore the crate prior to locking him in is an easy way to take away some of the crating fear factor. In a perfect world, you have a few days to introduce your pup to the crate, during which you don't have to lock him up and leave him there while you leave the house.

To acclimate the puppy gradually, place the crate in a central location in the house, leave the door open, and put a few savory treats inside. Praise the pup when he goes inside to eat the treats, and then allow him to exit the crate again. Continue planting treats inside the crate for the pup to discover throughout the day. Then place a few interesting toys inside the crate and lock the door so that your pup can see and smell the goodies but can't get to them. You can even anchor a treat-stuffed toy in the back of the crate so

Accelerated Crate Info

You just brought your new puppy home, and there's no time to do a slow crate acclimation. What now? First, do your best to wear out your pup before bedtime. She's more likely to tolerate the first night of crating if she's so tired that she can't keep her eyes open. Take a walk, play hard, and try not to let your puppy fall asleep on the couch before crate time. Take her on a potty trip and watch to see that she actually goes, and then put her in the crate with a hard rubber treat-stuffed toy. (Test out the toy beforehand to ensure that your pup can't rip pieces off of it.) Keep the crate close to wherever you are, and be prepared to take her out for another potty trip again if she wakes up. You'll probably hear a few protest whimpers when you first put her inside, but if you did your best to wear her out, sleep should soon follow.

that your puppy has to go inside in order to enjoy it. The goal is to create a comfortable, familiar, and rewarding place for your pup to hang out. Feeding your puppy her meals in the crate will help as well. Begin by placing the food bowls at the front of the crate near the doorway, and as your dog becomes more comfortable with eating near the crate, move the

Anchoring a toy with sturdy string in the back of your puppy's crate is an easy way to encourage him to hang out inside.

A well-stuffed activity toy will keep your puppy happy and occupied in his crate.

bowls farther inside until he's eating all the way inside. Close the door while he eats, but remain close by, and then open the door and let him out shortly after he finishes but before he begins to whine.

Once your dog is entering the crate willingly, let him wander in to eat some of the planted treats, and then shut the door. Stay close by, and then let him out after a few minutes, before he vocalizes or attempts to get out. (If you've taken your time with the initial introductory steps, your pup probably won't be distressed about getting locked inside.) Repeat the process several times throughout the day, increasing the length of time your puppy remains in the crate. You can sweeten the deal by giving your puppy a special treat-stuffed toy while he's inside. A hard rubber activity toy that's stuffed with something novel like peanut butter or a small taste of soft cheese is hard to resist, and it's likely that your puppy won't even notice that the door is shut! When your puppy is occupied with the toy inside his crate, leave the room, and then come back after a few minutes, as always, before he vocalizes to get out.

It helps to put the puppy in the crate when he's already tired from a good romp. Make sure that he has had ample opportunity to potty outside (both kinds!), and then place him in the crate with a treat-stuffed activity toy. Lock the door and leave the room. Your puppy will probably work on the toy for a while and then fall asleep.

Consider Your Puppy's "Hold Time"

So how long can your puppy hold it? The rule of thumb is that the puppy's age in months roughly translates to the number of resting hours he can hold it. So a ten-week-old puppy can probably remain in the crate for about two hours without needing a potty break. (It's an inexact science that doesn't apply after about six months, so don't rely too heavily on the computation.) Smaller breeds have smaller bladders, and they typically skew to shorter "hold times." The sleeping puppy might be able to hold it for longer periods, so there's no need to wake your puppy in the middle of the night to take him out. When the urge strikes, your pup will let you know!

Crate training a puppy while you work full time is a challenge, as young pups *cannot* hold it for eight hours. Keeping a puppy in a crate that long is cruel and will completely ruin your dog's instinct to keep her den clean. If you're out of the house for longer than your puppy can comfortably hold it, either find a dependable friend or family member who can let your puppy out at the appropriate intervals, or hire a professional dog walker. If those options aren't possible (which would lead me to recommend that you adopt an older dog and not a puppy), you can attempt a long-term confinement scenario, which is described in the next section of this book.

Keep the Crate in a Central Location

We all know that crates aren't pretty and are space-wasters. It's tempting to hide your puppy's crate in a far-off room to keep it out of the way, but that plan usually backfires. The crate needs to be placed so that you can hear your puppy if she vocalizes to go out for a potty, which typically means keeping it in the kitchen or family room for daytime hours, and in the bedroom at night. You have to find a balance, though, so that your puppy is crated closely enough to you to be a part of your daily life, but not so dead-center that she can't rest because of the commotion.

Most very young puppies can't hold it for the entire night, so it's necessary that you are close enough to the crate to hear the pup when he wakes. Resist the temptation to bring your snuggly puppy into bed with you after a late-night potty trip. Your pup needs to continue to acclimate to the crate, so

Put your puppy's crate in an area of the house that's not completely secluded.

finish up that potty trip and take her directly back to it for a few more hours of sleep! If keeping the crate in your bedroom is impossible because of space constraints, keep a baby monitor near the crate so you can hear when it's time. If you don't hear your pup when she wakes, she might be forced to soil her crate, which could lead to more crate-training backsliding.

Keeping the crate in a central location also reinforces the idea that your puppy is a part of the family. Your puppy can get used to the rhythms of the household if he's actually close enough to be a part of them. Plus, it's important for a puppy to realize that going in the crate doesn't always mean that you're leaving him completely alone. The crate should be used if you're unable to give your dog your full attention, as was the case with Jane when she was on the computer. Crating comes in handy when you need to take a shower, prep dinner, help with homework, or be otherwise engaged. It's healthy to give your dog a chance to rest on his own. The crate can go mobile—it's perfectly fine to move it throughout the house as your day unfolds.

Make Release from the Crate No Big Deal

When it comes time to let your puppy out of her crate, remain low-key. Keep in mind that your pup is probably holding it, and your excited greeting might cause her to lose control of her bladder. Puppies don't have the bladder capacity and control of older dogs, which is why many pups piddle when they meet someone new. (More on that topic later!) Plus, you don't want her to think that getting *out* of the crate is the best part of crating. Release from the crate should be calm and quiet, to prevent accidents and reinforce the idea that there's nothing negative about being inside.

Is Remedial Crate Training Possible?

Your puppy or adolescent rescue dog has already decided that the crate is a scary place. Is it too late to change that perception? It depends on a few factors. First, just how dramatic was your dog's refusal to crate? Some dogs are acutely uncomfortable being in the crate because of past experiences. Those dogs might consistently use the crate as a bathroom instead of a "hold space" (although some dogs might eliminate in the crate because they have too much room), vocalize continuously and dramatically, or worse yet, self-injure in an attempt to escape. The crate is supposed to serve two purposes: preventing the dog from pottying inside the house and keeping the dog safe when unsupervised. If the crate is not fulfilling those duties,

Deciphering Crate Barks

Puppies often bark and whine when they're crated, so it's important to decipher the difference between an "I'm-bored-let-me-out" bark and a "Oh-my-gosh-I-gotta-go-out" bark. First, consider the context of the bark. Did you just put your dog in the crate and she's now vocalizing? That's probably a distress or boredom bark (unless you forgot to take your dog out prior to crating her). Has your puppy been in the crate for an hour and she's waking up from a nap? That's a potty bark. Don't let your dog out of the crate while she's barking—wait for a brief lull in the vocalization and *then* let her out so that she doesn't learn that barking "works." If you take your dog out and she would rather play than potty, take her inside again and put her back into the crate. Keep in mind, you will interpret your dog's barks incorrectly from time to time, and that's okay.

meaning the dog is consistently pottying in the appropriately sized crate or is harming itself trying to get out, it makes sense to discontinue the use of the crate. The uncrated dog, however, still needs boundaries, like baby gates and keen supervision.

It's possible to potty and chew train without using a crate, but it's a *lot* more work. You're basically on "dog duty" twenty-four hours a day, unless your dog is sleeping. I know of what I speak, as Olive considered her crate her own personal toilet no matter how restricted the space inside. We gave up the crate after four messy days, and from that point on I was her shadow. When I took a shower or was otherwise occupied in the bathroom, she was in the bathroom with me. She was tethered (on a leash that was attached to a heavy piece of furniture) in a safe spot in view when it came time to cook or eat a meal. We closed off the first floor of our house, using a mix of baby gates and old fireplace grates. Any time she stepped away from me my mantra was, "Olliive, where are you going?" When we left the house, both Olive and our resident dog, Millie the Smooth Brussels Griffon, were gated in a small bathroom. Because this "den" wasn't small enough to force her to keep it clean (an instinct that was broken anyway), she frequently had accidents in there. My days were ruled by Olive's elimination habits. I knew from experience that crate-assisted potty training, done correctly, is usually quick and easy. Unfortunately, because we couldn't use the crate (and also because of some of Olive's strange quirks), what should have taken a few weeks took about six months.

There's still hope if your dog is merely *intolerant* of being in the crate and not completely opposed to it as Olive was. If you have an airline crate

The clicker makes training seem like a game. It's effective, efficient, and fun!

and your dog is uncomfortable being in it, consider trying a wire one instead. For some dogs (and their lucky owners) this switch is all it takes. Another easy fix is moving the crate to a more central location in your home. If these changes don't help, training can save the day!

I'm a devoted clicker trainer. The clicker, a small matchbook-sized plastic device, is a very precise way of marking an appropriate behavior. It's a quick way of saying, "That's it! You did it correctly!" The click is quickly followed by a high-value food reward that reinforces the behavior that has just occurred. One of the coolest parts of clicker training is that it can mark tiny nuances and gestures that can be built into a completed behavior. You don't have to wait for your dog to go all the way in the crate to start rewarding him; in the early training stages, something as fleeting as a glance toward the crate can earn your dog a treat! This ability is invaluable when it comes to de-stressing the crate; rather than forcing your dog to enter the crate and work from a place of distress, you can click and treat components of that behavior while the dog is outside the crate, and slowly build those small behaviors into the finished product. It's a gentle, dog-friendly way of helping dogs to overcome fears, and it empowers both participants. Conquering crate fears with this method trains the behavior of going into the crate, and, more important, changes a dog's emotional reaction to crating. Instead of the crate being a place of fear, it's transformed into a place of fun!

To crate train with a clicker, first grab some special meaty treats and "charge" your clicker by clicking and then immediately follow up with a treat. Your dog doesn't have to do anything but keep all four paws on the ground. After about six to eight repetitions, your dog will probably understand that the click predicts a treat. Work on some basic sits with the clicker as well so that the clicker has a positive association with something easy for your puppy to do. Ask your dog to "sit," click when his rump hits the ground, and then give him a treat.

Now move closer to the crate. This is where you need to really tap into your observational skills, as you're going to be clicking and treating "approximations" of going into the crate, meaning the beginning stages of the process. If your dog even glances at the crate, click and treat! After several repetitions of rewarding for glances, require your dog to do a little more in order to earn the treat. Your dog might glance at the crate, and when you withhold the click, she might lean her body toward it, or even take a step toward the crate as if to say, "Hey, didn't you see what I just did?" At that point, click and treat!

Continue to raise the bar on what you click and treat. If you keep clicking the same behavior over and over (like when your dog takes a baby step toward the crate), that's all your dog will offer because she's working just to earn a treat. That said, withholding the click might make your dog frustrated. Be generous with clicks and treats during the early stages of crate training, particularly because your dog already has baggage about crating. Again, this exercise requires keen powers of observation, as many of your dog's movements will be fleeting. The clicker's precision allows you to communicate clearly to your dog what's working to earn her a treat.

Prepare for potential backslide that might come when your dog gets closer to the crate doorway. Crossing the threshold of the crate is a big deal for crate-sensitive dogs. Once your dog is comfortable offering you

Standing behind the crate is an easy way to "cheat" as your puppy learns to play the crate game.

behaviors close to the crate door, it helps to click your dog for moving even closer to it, and then drop the treat into the very front of the crate. You're not luring your dog all the way in with the treat ("Here's the treat, Fido, now go in!"); you're actually clicking to acknowledge your dog's forward movement and then stacking the deck in your favor by placing the treat in a place where she has to make even *more* forward movement in order to retrieve it! This "cheat" move often helps dogs conquer their initial fear of stepping in. Once your dog crosses the threshold with confidence—and yes, you'll be able to tell when that happens—drop the treat a little farther back into the crate every time you click instead of just handing it to your dog.

Your dog might have a "lightbulb" moment at this point, where she seems to say, "Oh! You want me to go in here! I get it!" From that point on, place the treat inside the crate and then stand behind it so that she'll have to go all the way in in order to collect. Clever dogs usually realize that if they stay in the crate, they'll continue to get clicks and treats. If that happens (and what a wonderful problem to have), click your dog for going in the crate, and then toss the treat just outside the mouth of the crate so that she has to exit the crate in order to collect. The hope is that she'll turn right back around and get in the crate again! Now you can name the behavior by associating a word with it that means, "Get in your crate." Pick a word like "home" or "crate" and say it as she crosses the threshold to go in. With enough repetitions your dog should be happily entering the crate when you begin playing the game.

After your dog has mastered going into the crate, add some time in between the moment she enters the crate and when you click. In a perfect world, your dog will enter and either sit or lie down. (This often happens naturally.) Making your dog wait patiently in the crate before she gets her click and treat reinforces the idea that being content in the crate makes good things happen. Praise your dog for entering and then pause before you click and treat. You can build up to a few minutes before you click and treat, and work up to leaving the room briefly before you click and treat.

Keep the crate-training sessions short and fun; take no longer than ten minutes initially. If possible, during the crate retraining process, don't crate your dog while you're away from the house as it's likely you'll lose progress if your dog is forced to go in the crate. You can prep your dog for hanging out in the crate long-term by finishing a training session with a well-stuffed treat-dispensing toy inside the crate. Let your dog enjoy it for ten to fifteen minutes while you go about your business in the next room, and then come back and let your dog out. Take the toy away so that your dog understands that she only gets the goodies when she hangs out in the crate.

This remedial training program won't help *every* dog, but I've seen it change many dogs' perspectives about crating. You can even use this method to train any dog to "kennel up" when you ask, not just crate-phobic dogs. It's a fun way to turn something your dog perceives as unpleasant into something that seems like a game. It takes time and dedication to rewire a dog's reaction to crating, but it's well worth the effort!

Home-Alone Trials

After you're convinced that your dog understands the potty rules as well as the chew rules (more on the rules in upcoming chapters), you can begin "home-alone and out-of-the-crate" trials. Unfortunately, there is no rule of thumb for the age at which a dog can be trusted out of his crate or long-term confinement space. That said, it's unlikely that a dog under six months old is fine-tuned enough to manage full household access while alone. When you're confident that your dog is ready for a little more freedom because she hasn't had an accident in the house or chewed anything inappropriate, begin by completely puppy-proofing the home, and then give your dog a stuffed activity toy and leave the house for ten minutes. If you return and nothing is out of place, celebrate! Next, start taking slightly longer trips away, perhaps fifteen to twenty minutes, always making sure to give your dog something constructive and safe to chew on before you leave. Continue lengthening the amount of time you're away from the house, making sure when you return that your dog hasn't been secretly chewing chair legs or eating toilet paper!

two

POTTY TRAINING

Potty training is hands down the number-one goal of new puppy ownership. No one wants to live with a dog that uses the family room rug as a toilet! Unfortunately, having housetraining problems is a typical reason for dog relinquishment to shelters, which is tragic as it's an entirely preventable problem. The techniques for teaching a new puppy where to potty are straightforward, but they require a great amount of dedication from pet families during the early stages. The good news is that consistency and repetition will make the job easier for both ends of the leash.

Case Study: Martin was admittedly unprepared when he rescued Molly the terrier mix. He was at a farmer's market and came upon a rescue organization showcasing a litter of six adorable eight-week-old pups just transported from a southern state. Martin stopped for a few minutes to pet the small spotted dogs, and before he knew it Molly "picked" him when she curled up on his lap and went to sleep. Martin had been thinking about getting a dog, but he didn't realize how quickly one would literally fall into his lap.

Martin had never had a puppy before. His only dog, Busby the lab mix, had been an adult "hand-me-down" dog from a friend who had to move. Busby was a mellow, full-potty-trained six-year-old when Martin inherited him, so he never had to go through the potty-training rite of passage. Martin mourned for two years after Busby died before he was ready to even think about another dog. He brought Molly the rescue pup home with the best of intentions but a lack of forethought, hoping that she would mirror Busby's seamless incorporation into his world. He soon discovered that his new puppy was nothing like his former dog.

Molly eliminated in the house constantly, or at least that's how it seemed to Martin. Initially she'd squat in front of him when she had to go but stopped after he began yelling at her for doing it. Instead, she opted to potty in rooms Martin seldom used, so it took days for him to discover her accidents. The messes drove fastidious Martin crazy. He knew from his experiences with Busby that dogs obviously need to go out after eating, but it always seemed like Molly had a postmeal accident before he had a chance to take her out. Martin couldn't understand why Molly always

Lessons Learned

Long ago people were told that shoving a puppy's face in his accident was an effective way to potty train a puppy. This outdated advice is wrong on many levels. First, it's a punitive way of trying to teach a lesson to a student who is still learning the rules. Grabbing your puppy and thrusting his face in his own waste is confrontational, and doing so can damage the growing bond you have with your dog. He won't understand what he did to make you angry, he'll just come to realize that you are unpredictable and scary. Additionally, your dog won't make the association between his act of elimination and your correction. If you happen to catch your puppy pottying in the house, interrupt him with a quick "Eh!" and then hurry him outside to complete the job. If you discover a puddle or a pile after the fact, consider it *your* mistake, not your puppy's.

walked away from their games of tug or fetch to go to potty in the hallway. He was smart enough to realize that spanking Molly for pottying inside was wrong, but he still walked her over to the messes and thrust her face close to them, yelling, "No! Molly, no! Bad!"

Martin didn't believe in crate training—he didn't understand the purpose of it—so Molly had the run of his condo. Martin could predict *where* she would eliminate (she liked the area rugs scattered around), but he couldn't seem to stop it from happening. When he left the house, he locked her in his bedroom to keep the messes contained. Molly usually had at least one accident every time Martin was away, often on his bed. He was sure she was doing it because she was mad at him for leaving.

Martin took Molly outside for walks three times a day. He was desperate for the young dog to burn through her pent-up energy. He usually took a short gravel path that led to tennis courts, where he let her off her leash to play fetch. The intense game typically lasted about fifteen to twenty minutes, and then the pair would return to the condo. It drove Martin crazy that nearly every time they came in from playing, Molly had an accident. He couldn't understand why, after spending so much time outside, she chose to potty inside. Martin was beyond frustrated with his puppy.

Possible Outcome One: Martin decides to get serious about the potty situation with Molly. Instead of allowing her to have the run of the condo, he opts to keep her locked behind a baby gate in his laundry room most of the time. He convinces himself that she's happier in the small room since she no longer gets yelled at for having accidents everywhere. (She still has accidents, but they're easier to clean up on the tile floor.) Martin occasionally allows her to hang out with him in the kitchen after playing outside. He feels a little bad about making Molly stay in the laundry room so much, but he believes that he can't trust her after all of the accidents she's had everywhere in his home. He wants to move to a house with a yard (where Molly could spend all of her time instead of the laundry room), and Martin wants to make sure to get his pet deposit back when he moves out of the condo. The stains all over the floor will make that difficult.

Possible Outcome Two: After months of frustrating accidents, Martin starts to seriously rethink his decision to bring Molly into his life. She has ruined two rugs, and he feels that his condo always smells like urine. He doesn't understand why Molly refuses to potty outside. He thinks the dog is spiteful and dominant because of her nonstop marking in the house. Martin feels that he did everything he could to housetrain Molly, it's just that she was either too stubborn or too stupid to figure it out. He finally decides that he can no longer tolerate a dog that has no respect for his authority, so he brings her to a nearby shelter.

This sad story is far too common. Though Martin felt that he did everything he could to potty train Molly, the truth is that he didn't even come close to getting the job done correctly. How should things have gone instead?

Create Predictability

Dogs thrive on routines. Establishing consistent meal, play, and potty times will help your dog get a sense of the patterns of daily life. Keeping your dog on a schedule will also keep *you* on track; if you know when the food goes into your dog, you'll have a better idea as to when it will need to come out! In Martin's case, he was used to his adult dog's rhythms after meals. He didn't understand that puppies need to go out from as soon as five minutes to as long as twenty minutes after eating.

Schedule hourly potty trips during your pup's initial weeks home. Creating a potty time worksheet will help to keep everyone in your household literally on the same page. Write down the time of the potty trip and what came out, if anything. Because of their small bladders, puppies need to eliminate frequently: after meals, after naps, and after—or even during—vigorous play. (This is why Molly often walked away from Martin and pottied when they played together.)

Schedule your puppy's mealtimes as well. Give her fifteen to twenty minutes to finish her food, and then pick up her bowl even if she left something behind. Leaving the bowl down for "free feeding" can prolong the potty training process, as your puppy might graze and "fill up" throughout the day when you're not aware, and then need to potty off schedule.

Make time for a few play sessions throughout the day as well, even though you'll probably end up playing with your puppy all the time! Try to play close to the time in which your puppy will need to be crated, so that when you put her in, she'll be tired and ready to settle down for a nap. Of course, make sure to take her outside postplay so that she can potty before crate time.

Nonstop Supervision

Martin didn't keep an eye on Molly, so he had no idea what she was doing when she was out of the room. Dogs don't come hardwired knowing that we want them to potty outside; they just know that they need to go when they need to go. That's where a combination of constant supervision and crating comes in handy.

A new puppy either needs to be directly within your sightlines or in the crate. It's as simple as that. "Directly within your sightlines" means that you can see what your puppy is doing at all times. She's not around the corner, down the hall, or hiding in the closet. (Baby gates set up throughout the house will prevent the puppy from meandering away.) "Directly in your sightlines" also means that you are not otherwise occupied with the TV, the computer, or cleaning up. It's not easy to maintain this level of supervision at all times (take it from me—I know firsthand thanks to Olive!), so that's where the crate comes in. If you are unable to give your puppy your full and undivided attention, you should crate your puppy with an approved bone or activity toy, one that you've watched your dog enjoy and are certain that she cannot chip, rip, swallow, or otherwise destroy in your absence. A puppy that learns to soothe itself with a chew is a happy puppy indeed.

Supervision is also required when your dog is outside for a potty break. It's tempting to send your pup out the back door and hope that she does her business, but it's more likely that she'll spend her time investigating good smells in the grass and chasing birds. You *must* accompany your dog to the yard to make sure that she uses her outside time to potty, and more important, so that you're there to reward her for doing it in the correct spot. Many of my clients tell me that their dogs go out to the yard and then eliminate when they come back inside. "My dog is abnormal! He only pees inside even though I let him out all the time!" they tell me. The missing link to this story is whether the person actually saw the dog eliminating outside. It's more likely that the pup got distracted and forgot the reason for being outside, only to realize when he comes back to the boring indoors that he has to go! If you take your puppy out when you're *sure* she has to go and

You need to accompany your puppy outside to make sure that this actually happens!

she still doesn't squat, bring her back inside and crate her again for five minutes. Then take her outside and try again.

Leaving your dog alone in the yard for an extended period of time—for example, when you're away from the house—is not an effective way to potty train. Your puppy might resort to boredom behaviors like digging, barking, and trying to escape the yard, but it's unlikely that she'll determine on her own that she's out there to eliminate. Martin's idea to move to a house with a yard and leave Molly outside would not alleviate his potty-training problem at all. It would probably just lead to a lonely, destructive, unpotty-trained adult dog.

Long-Term Confinement

If you are unable to let your puppy out for potty breaks during the workday and you can't find someone to help out, you must offer your puppy a long-term confinement solution. Long-term confinement is different from the crate in that your dog is still confined to a small area, but she also has a place to eliminate if necessary. This scenario is not ideal, as it permits your dog to get used to pottying inside, but it's better than forcing your puppy to soil her crate.

A long-term confinement area is a wire playpen set up with your puppy's crate and a designated potty spot on the opposite end. The area should be

Is It a Potty-Training Problem?

Many pups dribble when they're excited. This doesn't mean that the puppy is lapsing on the housetraining process! Pups usually grow out of this type of excitement urination as their bladders mature, but there are steps that you can take to minimize the problem. First, keep greetings low key. Don't loom over your dog when you first see her. Squat down facing away from your puppy and let her approach at her own pace. Keep your voice low, and don't squeal. If reaching out to touch your puppy is the release trigger, offer a few small treats in your cupped hand while you remain squatted and looking away from her instead of reaching out to pet her. This way your dog is still making contact with you, but she's more engaged in eating the food than getting pee-inducing pats. Don't reprimand your puppy for dribbling. This is an unconscious behavior that your puppy has no control of, and punishing your puppy for it could cause the behavior to become more deeply rooted as a submission behavior. (Submissive urination is a deferential behavior, and is a dog's way of saying, "You are greater than I!") It's best not to make a big deal of excitement urination.

sized so that the crate is far enough away from the potty area so that it's not unpleasant for your puppy, but not so big that she can choose spots *other* than the potty spot. You can use potty pads or newspapers for the potty area, but I think it's best to use the substance that your puppy is used to eliminating on: grass. If the season permits, buy a roll of sod and cut it appropriately sized pieces (smaller for a little dog, larger for a big dog). If not, you can purchase plastic "stadium grass" at a local hardware store. (Keep in mind that this type of plastic grass is more similar to the real thing to us than to your puppy!) Place the sod or stadium grass in a low kitty-litter pan so that the dampness doesn't drain through onto your floor.

The pen should be set up so that the only comfortable place for your puppy to rest is the crate, which will reinforce the idea that the crate is a good place to hang out. Provide a small bowl of water in an unbreakable dish, as well as a variety of approved treat-dispensing toys to keep your dog constructively occupied in your absence.

Use a Potty Phrase

Teaching your pup to eliminate using a word or phrase not only helps during the potty-training process, but it also will continue to serve a purpose

It's the Yard or Nothing at All!

This is a common concern of new puppy owners. The pup is a pro at eliminating in the yard, but she holds it for blocks when out on a walk, and then potties in the yard after returning home. You can "reprogram" your pee-resistant pup by changing her schedule. Instead of taking her out to the yard after finishing a meal, clip on her leash and take her for a walk instead. You can also forgo the early morning first potty trip of the day in the yard for a walk around the block. (It helps to wear sweats to bed so you don't have to change prior to going out!) Using your potty phrase will also help remind your puppy what she should be doing in the unfamiliar place.

for your dog's entire life. Select a word that works for you and your family and say it when your pup begins to eliminate. (Some pet owners might balk at having to say "pee pee" for upwards of ten years, so choose wisely!) I've always used a combination of "hurry up" and "go ahead" with my dogs. Say it softly as your dog eliminates, as you don't want to interrupt the flow, and then follow up with a tasty food reward *immediately* after she finishes. Waiting until you get back inside to reward won't effectively communicate to your dog why she's getting the reward; she might think that the treat happens when she comes in the door, when in fact *you* think that you're rewarding her for pottying outside. An immediate treat in the yard post-potty will let your dog know that she gets paid when she potties in the yard. You're not rewarding the act of elimination (which feels good so it's self-reinforcing); you're rewarding the location.

In time, typically a few days to a few weeks, you'll be able to ask your puppy to potty instead of waiting for it to happen. Just say, "Fido, hurry, hurry!" and in an almost Pavlovian response your puppy will seem to say, "Why, yes, I *do* have to go!" and begin pottying. This is helpful for times when the weather is bad and neither of you feel like being outside, or when you're in an unfamiliar environment like a rest stop on the side of the road, and your dog isn't sure why you're standing around staring at her.

Play after Potty

After your puppy eliminates, take some time to play and explore with her outside. If you rush her inside right after she goes, she'll soon understand that the longer she waits to potty, the longer she gets to stay outside. (Which will probably make *you* frustrated: "Why isn't she going? I know she has to go!") In a perfect world, a potty in the yard means a tasty treat and then a chance to engage in some play with you.

Consider Your Dog's Potty Preference

Every dog has a preferred spot for elimination. That's why country dogs can't figure out what to do when they visit grass-free city streets. (I know of a dog that held her bladder for more than twenty-four hours when she went to New York because she couldn't find a grassy patch she liked!) Puppies establish this preference at a young age, and it's in your best interest to determine what your puppy's preference is, and encourage elimination there initially. Fall puppies might seek out leaves, spring puppies might look for fresh grass . . . the exact spot shouldn't be a major concern initially, you just want to make sure that it's outside and not inside! Olive likes to eliminate in dense undergrowth, so she usually wades into our flower beds until the plants (I'll be honest, they're actually weeds) encircle her. Sometimes, if she's feeling bold, she'll climb atop a low evergreen bush and potty there. It's a weird preference, but because of our initial difficulties potty training her, I didn't care where she opted to go. In our case study, Martin thought that he gave Molly ample time to eliminate outside when he took her to the tennis courts to play fetch, but Molly was used to pottying on grass. Because Martin took a gravel path to the paved court and never helped her learn to potty anywhere else but grass, she never had the

Encouraging a Location Preference

Your puppy might prefer to eliminate in your herb garden, but that's not a habit you want to encourage long-term. What should you do? First, put your puppy on a leash when you go outside, even if you have a fenced in yard. Take your puppy to the spot that you'd like her to use and say your potty phrase to encourage elimination. When she's finished, have an *extra* special reward for her (perhaps a bit of cheese instead of the regular dog biscuit), as well as a ton of praise. You don't want to discourage her from going anywhere outside during the very early stages of potty training, but you can make it plain to your dog that the extra good stuff happens when she potties in the "special spot." It's also a good idea to familiarize your pup and encourage her to eliminate on a variety of novel surfaces, like mulch, pebbles, or sand, so that she doesn't refuse to potty if her preferred substrate isn't available.

Sniffing is a major prepotty signal, but there are other more subtle hints that come before.

chance to go. That's why she always eliminated when she returned home; carpet had become one of her preferred potty surfaces.

Learn to Recognize Potty Signals

Puppies exhibit a variety of obvious indicators when they need to go, and many subtle ones as well. The obvious ones include pacing, circling, and sniffing the ground. By the time a puppy is exhibiting these signals it means that the chamber is full and ready to be emptied. A less obvious but universal potty indicator is walking away from the action. If you're trying to play with your pup and she keeps dropping the toy and leaving, or if she seems distracted, it means that she has to go out. Walking out of the room is yet another subtle indicator that a dog is ready for a break. Other predictors include barking, pawing (which is Olive's method of choice), jumping up and down, and, if you're lucky, looking toward the door Lassie-style.

You can teach your dog to give you an unmistakable potty signal by ringing a bell when she has to go out. Find a bell that both you and your dog can live with. (Some pups might get frightened by a bell that's too loud or big.) Christmas bells on a string work, or a "ring for service" deli counter–style bell. Hang the bells from the doorknob or position the service bell near the door that you use most frequently for potty breaks. Make sure it's in a location the dog can reach.

A Little Less Noise

Although I love using bells for potty training, I don't like hearing them clank against the door every time it opens. Hanging the bells from an adhesive hook right next to the door is a great alternative if you're sound-sensitive like me, plus it makes the bells more accessible for petite pups that can't reach them when hung from the doorknob.

When it's time for your puppy to go outside, gently clasp her paw and use it to tap the bells so that they make a sound. Immediately take your pup outside for the potty break. Continue to help your dog to ring the bells every time you go out for potty time. Don't use the bell when you go out to play, as you don't want your dog to start using the bell as a catch-all "lemme out" signal! Your puppy should soon understand that the bells predict the trip outside for potty, and will ring it on her own when she feels the need. Some trainers suggest giving your dog a treat for ringing the bells, but I prefer a treat-free methodology. Otherwise, the bell ringing will become more of a party trick to get a reward than an accurate potty predictor.

How fast can a dog learn to ring a bell? I have one client whose yellow lab picked it up in under a week, but the typical learning curve lasts about two weeks.

Accidents Will Happen

Despite your best efforts, it's possible your puppy still might have an occasional accident in the house. If you happen to catch your puppy in the act, interrupt her in such a way that it stops the flow but doesn't completely startle her. You want to stop her without giving her a complex about pottying when you're around. Immediately take your dog outside to complete the job, even if she was 90 percent done when you found her, and reward her for completing the job outside. If you discover the puddle or pile after the fact, do not, under any circumstances, punish your dog for it. Dogs don't view elimination the way we do—to them it's pretty darn interesting. Think about how much time they spend investigating the leavings of other dogs! Punishing your dog after finding a mess, as Martin did with Molly, will not make the point that messing in the house is against the rules, despite your dog's groveling when you shout at her. What looks like an admission of guilt is actually just your dog responding to your angry tone. Sadly, you can get that same reaction from your dog if you point to the ground and say, "Fido! Why did you breathe that air? Huh? *Why did you*

When Something Is "Off"

The puppy that seems impossible to housetrain might actually have an undiagnosed medical problem like a bladder infection. If you suspect that your dog's increased thirst, pacing, and house soiling are not normal, ask your vet to do a urine culture to ensure the proper antibiotic treatment if necessary. A puppy with consistently loose stool or diarrhea—she can't quite make it out the door in time—might have a parasite. Bring a stool sample to the vet for testing.

breathe?" (Not that I recommend scolding your dog for fun.) When you yell, the only thing you're teaching your dog is that you're unpredictable and scary.

If you find an accident, clean it up with a commercially available odor eliminator; most regular household cleaners contain ammonia, which mimics the scent of urine and might encourage your puppy to soil the same area. Then make sure to step up your supervision.

Grant Household Access Gradually

How do you go from complete lockdown in your home to giving your puppy a little more freedom inside? Once your puppy is becoming predictable with her potty habits, you should be able to take away a gate dividing two frequently used rooms, like the one between the kitchen and the family room. Removing a gate will grant additional access but still permit you to keep your puppy in sight. (The gate closing off the upstairs isn't a good place to start—too tempting!) Explore the room with your dog. As always, give your puppy something to keep her occupied while she's in the new space, like a treat-stuffed activity toy or bone.

In our scenario with Olive, we started with a series of gates set up throughout the house, the most annoying of which—a heavy iron fireplace screen—blocked off a high-traffic area near the couch. Olive had taken advantage of the spot behind the couch when my husband was on puppy-watching duty (he didn't take the job as seriously as I did), and I knew that I had to prevent access to avoid future mishaps. We kept that ugly, annoying screen up for months. Then, after a run of dry weeks, I got rid of it. I watched Olive carefully those first few days after I'd removed it and was happy to discover that the area no longer was of interest. It was the first and most welcome gate in our house to bite the dust!

Remedial Potty Training for Older Dogs

Potty training isn't always for young dogs with small bladders. Some adult rescue dogs come into their new homes unsure of proper potty protocol. If a dog is older than six months and still has the occasional accident in the house, she's not fully housetrained. The good news is that it's never too late to housetrain a new dog! The adult dog process is nearly identical to the puppy process, with the added benefit of fully developed bladder control.

Supervise and schedule: Adult dogs appreciate a predictable lifestyle as well. Scheduling meals, walks, nap times, and playtimes also allows for you to schedule potty times. Much like puppies, unhousetrained adult dogs need to be either supervised or confined, so don't allow your unhousetrained adult dog free run of the house. It's a common mistake to assume that a dog should be potty trained just because he's grown. If he never learned, he never learned, and he should be treated like a new puppy.

Crate if possible: Adult dogs with housetraining issues often have baggage associated with crating that goes far beyond what new puppies exhibit. Perhaps they were crated for too long and forced to soil their cage, or perhaps they've *never* been confined and it feels foreign to them. If one crate type doesn't work for your adult dog (meaning he soils in it or rebels dramatically), consider switching to a different type of crate, or use an exercise pen instead. If you're certain that your dog isn't destructive, you can baby gate him off in a small room like a guest bathroom. I prefer to put a baby gate across the door instead of closing the door, as it's less confining.

Even though adult dogs have greater bladder capacity, it doesn't mean that they should stay in the crate for the entire day. (Remember, the month-to-hour computation of "hold time" doesn't apply after six months.) Older dogs that aren't acclimating to the crate should follow the same protocol as pups, including eating meals inside, and special treat-stuffed activity toys during quiet time in the crate.

Accompany your dog outside: Much like potty-training puppies, you need to actually watch your adult dog to make sure that he has taken care of business in the yard. You might think that he knows what to do, but there's a good chance that he doesn't. (Don't forget, many adolescent dogs are relinquished to shelters because they weren't properly potty trained.) Take your dog out, start to use a potty phrase, and then reward immediately for a job well done.

Learn your dog's signals: Adult "I-gotta-go" signals are often more definitive than puppy signals. Look for pawing, barking, pacing, and general distractedness as indicators of the need for pee.

How Can I Tell If My Puppy Is Housetrained?

Your puppy has gone a week without an accident, so you're ready to dismantle the crate and get rid of the baby gates. Not so fast! You're definitely making progress, but a dry week is just the beginning of the journey to home plate. You and your puppy need to have a dry *month* before you can begin to consider her fully housetrained, and even then you shouldn't trust her 100 percent.

Keep in mind that you're using tools like the crate and baby gates for multiple reasons, not just for potty training. Baby gates keep your dog in sight and out of rooms that aren't puppy-proofed, crates and gates prevent household destruction, and the crate gives your puppy a quiet place to rest (and gives you peace of mind!). Don't put the equipment away until both ends of your puppy are predictable and trustworthy.

It's easy to write off the "now-and-then" accidents that happen when you think your dog is fully potty trained. One little pee in the house doesn't seem like a big deal after coping with multiple pees on your rugs for months. Unfortunately, every indoor accident is almost a guarantee of additional ones. If your puppy still has the occasional accident after you consider her fully trained, I've got news for you: she's not potty trained.

After many frustrating months, our Olive was finally potty trained. She now understands the potty word and eliminates when I ask. She lets me know that she has to go out by scratching at my leg and looking slightly crazed. (Sometimes those leg scratches are just pleas for more dinner!) I'll admit that her slow progress tested me, but in the end it made me an even more diligent potty trainer.

three

HOUSEHOLD DESTRUCTION

Puppies explore their world with their mouths, and if not properly directed, they can do some major damage with those sharp little teeth! A pup can't tell the difference between your antique hooked rugs and her favorite chew toy; all she knows is that she needs to put something in her mouth *now*. When a puppy meets the dangerous intersection of boredom and teething with no proper outlets, your home or your possessions will bear the brunt of the damage.

Case Study: Michelle's Shepherd mix Emmett was mouthy from the day she rescued him. The four-month-old dog always needed something in his mouth, whether it was a sanctioned tug toy or something forbidden, like Michelle's expensive shoes. (He loved to grab shoes and run through the house with the entire family chasing behind him.) Michelle knew that Emmett was at the beginning of the teething phase, so she did her best to provide him with numerous plush toys and a few hard rubber bones to keep him occupied. They didn't work for long; Emmett ignored the rubber toys and gutted and shredded the plush ones within minutes. Michelle was getting tired of his expensive habit. Sometimes he grabbed her children's toys, which led to tears and frustration. She couldn't understand why the toys she bought for him weren't working to keep him occupied, and she thought that he was being spiteful when he grabbed things that didn't belong to him.

Michelle tried to keep Emmett gated in the kitchen when she was home but not watching him, and crated when she was out of the house. She was doing a fine job with Emmett's potty training, but she just couldn't get a handle on his household destruction. Whenever he was quiet in another room, she knew that he was up to no good. Sometimes it was her children's shoes, sometimes it was couch pillows, sometimes it was a stack of magazines in the basket by her chair. It was always *something*, and there was so much available in her house for him to enjoy. Emmett seemed insatiable.

Possible Outcome One: On a particularly homework-fraught night, Michelle couldn't watch Emmett but forgot to put him in the kitchen. Her attention was focused completely on her daughter's complex fourth-grade diorama, so she didn't even hear the noises coming from the family room. Two hours later she walked in the room to find Emmett asleep, surrounded by an array of his spoils: two chewed-up remote controls, massively tooth-marked legs of her coffee table, frayed tassels on the edge of her area rug, and a confetti parade of yesterday's newspaper.

Possible Outcome Two: Emmett was known for his attraction to dirty laundry. He grabbed underwear and ran any chance he could get. The family did their best to keep their laundry out of reach, but it seemed like someone was always forgetting to close a door or laundry basket. One evening Michelle came home after being away for several hours to discover a single sock lying close to Emmett. The other was missing. Had he eaten it? A worrier by nature, Michelle called her vet for advice. At his suggestion she induced vomiting using hydrogen peroxide, but the sock didn't come up. The vet told her it was okay to wait until morning to see if Emmett passed it or threw it up. The next day Emmett refused breakfast so she packed him up and headed to the vet office. Her hunch was right on; Emmett had indeed ingested the sock. The veterinarian told Michelle that the size and position of the sock wouldn't allow it to pass naturally, so they had to remove it surgically.

Unfortunately, these are common scenarios. The combination of a chew-crazy puppy and a household filled with exciting contraband can lead to anything from general destruction to surgical procedures. How could Michelle and her family have prepped for the arrival of Hurricane Emmett? Let's rewind.

Puppy-Proof the House

An active puppy can find her way into all sorts of trouble. A bored, unsupervised puppy is like a toddler without a diaper on carrying a tall glass of grape juice in a room with white carpet; there's a *lot* that can go wrong! Puppies can get very creative when they feel the need to chew, or even when they're just bored. The first step in preventing household calamities like the ones Michelle experienced with Emmett is creatively puppy-proofing your home. The best way to do that is to go room to room, starting down at your puppy's eye level and working up.

Kitchen: Look for cords and plugs that would be easy for your puppy to grab. Secure low drawers and cupboards with baby-proof locks, particularly if they contain household cleansers. Remove dangling towels and area rugs. Take a closer look at your garbage and recycling cans; open receptacles with intriguing smells are invitations to inquisitive puppies, so either put them in a space where your puppy can't reach them, or select cans that have sturdy lids. Secure cords to blinds and curtains, particularly ones that are low enough for your puppy to reach. Keep the cat food and litter box at a safe distance from your puppy, as many dogs can't resist sampling leftovers in the litter box! (An easy way to puppy-proof your litter box is to install a baby gate in the doorway a few inches above the floor, so that your cat can fit underneath but your puppy can't.)

Family room: As with the kitchen, secure electrical cords. Remove dangling pillows and blankets. Remove magazines and books on low coffee tables or in baskets on the floor. (Baskets are irresistible to puppies!) Place remote controls and curios on high shelves. Relocate any potted plants on the floor, as some plants are poisonous, and the dirt can be a temptation for diggers as well. Protect all furniture legs, which are an attraction to pups. Two of my clients found a low-cost way of stopping their Basset Hound puppy from chewing on their table and chair legs: they covered them with flexible white tubing from a hardware store. The plastic protected the furniture and added a modern look to her family room until the puppy was out of the chewing phase! Of course, if you like the look of your family room as is, you can always purchase a chew-deterring bitter spray for your furniture, following the directions on the bottle.

Bedroom: Keep laundry off the floor. Keep shoes in the closet with the doors shut. Don't leave throw pillows on the floor. Clean out under your bed, or block access so that your puppy can't get underneath. (Some puppies like to rip up the lining on the bottom of the bed.) Keep drawers completely closed. Watch out for loose change that might have fallen out of your pockets, as a curious puppy might swallow the coins.

Bathroom: You'll have to be particularly careful if you plan to keep your dog in the bathroom when you aren't home. Lock the cabinets under the vanity so your puppy can't get into your toiletries. Keep the toilet lid closed and the bath tissue high enough that your puppy can't grab it and run. Move the toilet brush and plunger to a secure location. Bathroom garbage can be especially tempting for puppies, so keep it out of sight or locked up. Watch out for soap, shampoo, and razors on the low ledge of the tub. It's a good idea to tuck your shower curtain on the inside of the shower if your puppy is unattended in the bathroom.

Laundry room: Put all cleaners, detergents, and bleach products high up or in a locked cabinet. Keep laundry off the floor. Close front-loading machines. Put brooms and mops in a closet. Pick up shoes.

No matter how thorough you are about puppy-proofing your home, there's always a chance that your creative puppy might find something to chew that you never considered a target. The goal, of course, is not only to proof your house but also to give your puppy enough chewing variety that he won't be interested in the sunglasses you accidentally left on the chair.

Teaching "Drop It"

If your puppy manages to grab your favorite T-shirt out of the laundry, resist the urge to chase her! Puppies *love* to be chased, and doing so will only encourage her to grab contraband more often in order to get the game going. Instead, get a high-value treat (you should have bowls of treats scattered throughout your home for situations like this one) and walk calmly toward your puppy. If you move too quickly, your pup will probably think that you're playing and take off! As you walk, praise your puppy for staying still, saying things like, "Look what you have! You found my favorite shirt! What a good girl!" Keep in mind that your puppy is still learning the difference between your stuff and her stuff. Even though it feels counterintuitive to praise your dog when she has contraband in her mouth, remaining calm will make her more likely to happily relinquish the object instead of taking off with it. When you're close to her, place the treat right in front of her nose and say "drop" as she opens her mouth to take the treat. Then praise her effusively! If your puppy sees you coming and then takes off (which is what a dog that has been chased before will probably do), run in the opposite direction of your puppy. Your curious pup will probably run after you. Take a handful of treats from one of the bowls you've wisely placed throughout your house and scatter them on the ground. When your pup drops the item in order to clean up the treats, quietly walk over and reclaim it.

Bones and chews will help to steer your puppy away from your stuff and to her own cache of goodies instead.

Provide Appropriate Chews

Michelle did her best to give Emmett the kinds of things she thought he might like to play with and chew. The problem is that the items she selected didn't appeal to Emmett's need to sink his growing teeth in and gnaw. Michelle thought they were great options, but Emmett *didn't,* and if the dog doesn't want to play with the sanctioned toys provided, he'll happily find other items that interest him! Plush toys are great for interactive play, meaning you and your dog play with them together, but they're not great for unsupervised time with a hyperdestructive dog. Most dogs get bored with plush toys and shred them because there is nothing else to do with them. Busy puppies like Emmett need something more to keep them constructively occupied, and that's where treat-stuffed activity toys can save the day again.

Pack It Up

Using a different treat stuffer can make an old toy seem new! Peanut butter is the go-to stuffer, but there are many more options. You can also stuff toys with:

- cheese in a can
- low-fat cream cheese
- frozen chicken broth
- layered biscuits
- unsweetened applesauce
- canned pumpkin
- canned dog food
- banana
- novel kibble
- cheese chunks
- apple slices
- baby carrots

It's imperative to have a variety of treat-stuffable hard rubber toys available for your puppy. There are limitless options available, ranging from those with super-simple treat-delivery systems to toys that provide

Treat-stuffable toys are a great way to keep a busy pup focused and happy.

The variety of chew bones available is astounding. Some are better than others, though.

Bones and chews: Nearly every animal body part can be utilized as a chew, from the tips of antlers to ears, snouts, kneecaps, and hooves. The consistency and longevity of these body parts vary greatly, so let's bone up on bones.

Bully sticks: The King of Bones, beloved by nearly every dog. Bully sticks are made of . . . well . . . the part of a bull that makes him a bull. Bully sticks are among the most expensive dog chews. Lower-cost bully sticks usually have a pungent aroma, while the pricier versions have been treated to remove odors. Bully sticks don't stain or make a mess. They come in a variety of lengths and thicknesses, typically from about three inches to twelve and over. Bully stick longevity varies, but the rule of thumb is the thicker the stick, the longer the chew. The entire stick is consumable, and most dogs chew on them until the end is a white pulpy mess—it's rare that a dog breaks off large chunks. It's best to take the bully stick away when it's a quarter of its original size. Many dogs that manage to swallow the last "too-big-to-swallow" piece of bully stick digest and pass it naturally. There are exceptions that require surgical intervention, however, like the Clumber Spaniel I worked with years ago that swallowed a six-inch stick whole. Supervision and offering a "treat for a trade" when the bone looks small can help to avoid swallowing issues.

Treated marrow bones: Marrow bones are an excellent low-cost chew for puppies and adult dogs. These hollow bones typically range from two inches up to ten inches. Some are treated so that they are a bright white, while others maintain some of their natural color and marrow within. Because marrow bones, like all bones, are a natural product, there is great variation within the thickness of the wall of the bone. Some can withstand the jaws of the toughest chewer, while other bones might crack under the pressure. As always, supervision will enable you to determine the best type of marrow bone for your puppy. The "mess factor" of marrow bones depends on the type you select; the treated white bones are tidy, but the meaty marrow bones can leave some crumbs. They're not usually greasy, and they don't stain. Marrow bones are a "renewable resource," as they can be restuffed with peanut butter or any of the other goodies listed on page 45.

Antlers: Deer, moose, and elk antlers are recent additions to the natural-chew market. The antlers are naturally shed, either by farm-raised animals or wild ones. Because of that, antlers are pricey chews. They have no smell, and they don't stain. Antlers are among the toughest chews available, so they're a good fit for aggressive chewers. The size ranges dramatically, both by the weight of the antler to the length of it. Moose antlers are typically large and flat, almost like dinner plates with crown points along the edge. Deer and elk antlers look very similar, though my anecdotal research suggests that elk antlers are harder and longer lasting. Not every dog enjoys a super-hard chew, though, because there's no easy "payoff," so some dogs don't bother with them. Both elk and deer antlers are available in "splits," meaning the antler has been cut in

Olive enjoys the King of Bones—the bully stick.

continues

half lengthwise, exposing the marrow within. Some dogs prefer the easier-to-chew split antlers over the whole ones. Antlers are among the longest-lasting chews available, but some dogs still manage to shave them down quickly. It is possible that pieces of antler can break off, so like any bone or chew, supervise your dog.

Pig ears: Pig ears are a low-cost chew option. They're exactly what they sound like (and look like): the treated ear of pig. Pig ears are a greasy chew that can leave some residue on lighter carpets. They're rapidly consumable—some dogs finish them off in a few crunches—and are very rich. Because of that, pig ears don't agree with every dog's digestive system. Their quick consumption and potential for tummy upsets rank pig ears as an occasional treat, not a go-to chew.

Long bones: Long bones are any other bones that aren't hollow in the middle, and include body parts like femurs, ribs, shanks, patellas, and knuckles. They're typically low-to-medium-cost chews, and can range anywhere from six inches to more than fourteen inches. Like marrow bones, they usually have bits of marrow on them and can be a little greasy if the dog doesn't clean up the remnants that fall off. Though they are heavy and often look like prehistoric dinosaur bones, long bones like femurs and rib bones can be less stable than hollow marrow bones. I've seen medium-sized dogs chew the rounded edges off of a femur bone, and I've witnessed dogs of all sizes, from Jack Russell Terrier up to Labs, cracking through a long thin rib bone in minutes. Long bones are best for less-aggressive chewers.

more of a challenge for the experienced puzzler. With novice pups, it helps to start with a toy that gives an easy payout. As your puppy learns how to "unpack" activity toys, you can begin offering more difficult options. (Any time you switch to a new toy, make it easy for your dog to unpack it the first time to prevent frustration.)

A common complaint about activity toys is that once dogs figure out how to get the treats out, they can unpack them within minutes, thereby negating the "keep-your-dog-constructively-occupied" concept. The secret is in the stuffing! Putting a single biscuit inside or just a tablespoon of peanut butter isn't a challenge and won't keep your puppy busy for long. Once your puppy understands how to play with an activity toy, you should pack it so that it takes time and effort to get the goodies out. If you're using biscuits, layer them side by side so that they form a wall of deliciousness. If you use something messy, like applesauce or pumpkin, freeze it.

Other body parts: Most remaining body parts are more rapidly consumable than the ones listed above. Snouts, tracheas, tendons, pig skins, and hooves can be great novel chews, but they don't provide the "hang time" you get with harder bones.

Not recommended: Rawhide is a go-to chew option that needs to be retired. Cheap grocery store rawhide is usually processed overseas, with questionable safety and handling procedures. (Harsh chemicals are often used to achieve that bright white look.) Rawhide presents a substantial choking hazard, as dogs can chew off large pieces, like the end of a knotted rawhide "bone," and the pieces can become lodged in the dog's throat. Though compressed rawhide, which is small bits of rawhide combined with a binding agent, is safer from a choking perspective, it's too soft to provide the resistance a growing puppy needs in order to exercise its jaws. If your dog can't live without her rawhide chews and you're comfortable with the associated risks, look for USA-made products that aren't colored and don't contain artificial flavorings.

The decision to give your dog a bone or chew is a personal one. You should understand the potential risks of cracked teeth, swallowed fragments, or splintered bone shards, and select your dog's chews accordingly. Safety always comes first; as I've mentioned, supervise your dog when you offer a new bone or chew, take it away if you can't be with your dog, and wash up after handling any bone or chew. In my twenty years of dog guardianship I've never had a problem with giving my dogs bones, but I do recognize that accidents happen. It's a risk I'm willing to take—but what you do is up to you.

Many people ask, "How will my dog get everything out if it's packed so well?" Determined dogs can get pretty creative, and I've heard stories of dogs repeatedly throwing the stuffed toy on the ground to jar treats loose, or carrying the toy to the top step so that goodies fall out as it rolls down. If your dog can't manage to get every morsel out, soak the toy in water to break down whatever is left, and then wash it using a bottle cleaner.

In addition to activity toys, I love giving puppies chew bones. There are many veterinarians, however, who don't approve of them because of the bone possibly splintering and the dog getting cut by shards, or a tooth cracking on the bone. While there is no bone or chew that is *100 percent* guaranteed safe, I feel that the risk is worth the rewards. Bones are an easy, tasty way to keep a busy dog content and anchored, allowing you to go about your day without having to worry, "What is the puppy destroying now?" Plus, bones are an excellent way for pups to exercise their jaws and deal with the discomfort of new teeth erupting.

Every dog has a different chewing style; some are tenacious bone crunchers, while others gnaw on the bone until it's a pulpy mess. The first step in determining if *your* puppy can safely chew on bones is to watch her attempt it with one. (Again, you should supervise your dog any time you give her something new.) Select a size-appropriate bone, meaning one that is too large for your puppy to swallow whole but not so big that she can't manage it. Then watch and listen as she chews. If you can hear the bone cracking, take it away immediately. If your puppy chews without cracking the bone or attempting to ingest the entire thing in one gulp, you can let your puppy enjoy the ride. Keep in mind as your puppy grows and develops, her chewing style will change as well.

Provide Ample Exercise

It's almost too obvious to state: puppies have boundless energy. There is no off switch on a growing puppy, which can lead to frustration when your puppy still wants to go-go-go even after you come back from a twenty-minute walk. It takes much more than a quick stroll to take the edge off of a puppy's energy. Bored, underexercised puppies are more likely to find their own ways to expel pent-up energy, like the grab-and-dash game Emmett played with his family, as well as the shoe, carpet, and table chewing. Emmett's people led very busy lives, and even though they thought he was getting enough exercise during their three daily walks, they barely put a dent in his energy levels. In positive dog-training circles, it's now controversial to say, "A tired dog is a good dog," but the statement rings true even with its anti-politically-correct phrasing.

The puppy that never seems to settle down and is always getting into mischief is the puppy that probably isn't getting enough exercise. The good news is that for most puppies, you don't need a three-acre yard and a herd of sheep to tire them out. Although there are some exceptions, a few pant-inducing games and a little bit of brain work are usually enough to wear out even the most spring-loaded puppy. The benefits of a properly worn-out dog are numerous: your puppy will probably be more than happy to take a nap in her crate, she'll emerge from her nap rested and at a lower "baseline," and the games you play together will strengthen the growing bond between the two of you.

One of my favorite ways to tax Olive's brain and body is to do some quick clicker-training sessions with her. She's incredibly food driven and she loves to play, so the opportunity to "work" for food makes her dance with anticipation. She's *so* food driven that when we play-train I use a dry kibble that isn't her normal dog food, which is actually a pretty boring treat. She loves it! Not every dog will work for kibble, though, and my kibble use with Olive is situational. When we're working on more important behaviors, like sit for greeting or coming when called, I use super-savory treats like cheese or chicken.

Play-training can incorporate the basic training you're already doing with your puppy, like "sit" and "down," but should focus more on fun nonessential behaviors, like "roll over" or "shake." If you're teaching your puppy "go to your crate" as described in the previous chapter, use the same steps to transition the behavior to her bed. "Go to bed" is a useful cue because you can use it to keep your puppy from underfoot, and it's *really* adorable. There's nothing sweeter than a puppy that races to her bed when you ask! This cue, though fun to teach and use, is actually one of the more mentally taxing basic behaviors to master. It requires that the trainer have excellent observational skills, as well as a puppy that is willing to be creative and try out new behaviors. As with the crate training, the trainer needs to use the clicker and treats to capture even the slightest approximation of the finished behavior, like a glance toward the bed, or a baby step toward it, and then build those increments to the finished product. I once worked with a French Bulldog puppy that translated our simple request to "go to bed" to mean "leap a foot in the air and then onto your bed." Even though we didn't teach her to jump on her bed as if clearing a hurdle, she did it every time, and we all laughed at her gleeful performance. It only took about six repetitions of this brain-busting behavior from different parts of the room to get her panting!

Playing rule-bound games with your puppy will also help to zap some of her manic energy. Mindful games—ones where you're an active participant instead of a zombie throwing a tennis ball, or ones where you inappropriately chase or wrestle with her—will do wonders to wear her out. One of my favorite games, tug, is still considered controversial in some circles. Trainers once believed that playing tug with dogs could make them "dominant" or aggressive, but playing tug with a few rules is a great way to burn pent-up energy in a small space. Plus, it helps to teach self-control and can bolster your pup's basic obedience training.

Tug: The rules of tug are simple: the puppy begins the game when I ask, drops the toy when I ask, and ends the game when I ask. Using rules helps to keep the game civilized and predictable, so that even the puppy that seems out of her mind with tugging excitement can reel in her energy level and perform a few simple training cues when you ask. You can teach the rules as you play—there's no need for formal training when it comes to tug time. To begin, find a tug toy you both can live with, meaning your dog likes the feel of it in her mouth, and you can hold on to it comfortably. (To avoid confusion, don't use household items like towels or socks.) Hold the toy out to your puppy and say, "Take it!" in a cheerful voice. Of course, your puppy won't know what the phrase means initially, but the context clues in your tone of voice, your body language, and the dangling toy in

Despite what you might have heard, playing tug with your dog won't make her aggressive!

front of her face will probably clue her in! When she latches on, tell her "good girl!" and hold on!

Avoid wrenching your puppy's head up and down or side to side as she tugs, as this can injure her neck. Keep your hand stationary and let her set the pace for tugging. Don't be concerned if your puppy makes little growly noises as she tugs. It's normal! Both of my dogs sound like demons when they play tug, but the noises stop the second I ask them to drop the toy.

If your puppy works her way up the toy and bites your hand, shout "Ouch!" and let go of the toy and walk away. If your puppy drops the toy and follows you, reclaim the toy and take a break for a few minutes so that she can't grab the toy from your hands. Resume the game by asking her to "take it" once again. This brief time-out will teach your dog that the game ends if she puts teeth on skin, and will discourage further misfires in the future. (More on nipping and biting to come.)

Tug can be an excitable game for eager puppies, so it's important to take frequent breaks. To interrupt the game, take a small but savory treat and place it right in front of your puppy's nose. She will probably release the toy in order to eat the treat, so "name" the behavior by saying "drop it" right as your puppy opens her mouth to get the treat. Use this treat in front of the nose trick to encourage your puppy to drop the toy about a half dozen times, and then ask her to drop without making the treat so obvious. Say "drop it" and then give her the treat after she lets go of the toy. Once you have sole control of the toy, ask your puppy to do a quick sit. Wait for a few seconds of calm, and then ask your puppy to "take it." If your puppy grabs for the toy before you offer it, hide it behind your back for a few moments and then repeat the sit/take it sequence.

Continue playing the game as long as your puppy can refrain from nipping your skin and can drop and take it when you ask. You can incorporate another level of fun by asking your puppy to "drop it" and then ask for a sit, followed by throwing the tug toy across the room. Your puppy will probably retrieve it and bring it right back to you for more tugging fun. When you're ready to end play for the day, ask for the "drop" and then signal the end of play by saying something like "all done!" (This is another "teach-as-you-go" cue.) Put the toy away so that you can keep it special for playtime only.

Find it: My favorite brain-busting game to play with busy puppies is "find the toy." It's an excellent way to tap into your puppy's developing tracking skills. Select a toy that you know your puppy loves (a plush toy with a squeaker is a good fit) and show it to your puppy. Let your puppy see you place the toy somewhere just out of sight, and tell your puppy to "find it!" Get excited when she does, and play with her and the toy for a few minutes. Continue hiding the toy in obvious spots so that your puppy starts to understand that when you say "find it!" she needs to hunt for the toy. (Yet another "teach-as-you-go" cue.) Then have someone take your puppy out of the room and hide the toy so that she doesn't see where you're putting it. Place it in a spot you've previously used for this first blind-seek and then let her back in the room and tell her to "find it." You can help your puppy find the toy the first few times she tries looking for it, but refrain from offering too much help as she'll then rely on you instead of honing her senses to find it on her own. "Find the toy" can be played inside or outside, and it will wear out even the busiest puppies. You can use a treat-filled activity toy as the final "hide" to encourage your puppy to settle down and chew after an energetic round of play.

There are tons of other mindful games that you can play with your puppy to tire her out, but these are two of my favorites. The rules for any game you choose to play with your puppy should always revolve around constructive appropriate play by your pup, and gentle, consistent guidance from you. Any game that encourages inappropriate behavior like jumping up, biting, wrestling, or other out-of-control behavior should be avoided.

Schedule Puppy Play Dates

Nothing wears out a puppy like a canine buddy, and as I said before, a tired dog is a good dog. My little store often serves as the de facto puppy park, where new puppy parents bring their dogs to burn off energy with other like-minded pups. I was always thrilled when puppy visitors showed up at the store to play with young Olive, as the fifteen minutes she spent tearing around the displays usually resulted in an hour-long nap at least.

Finding the right sort of puppy pal is key. The dogs should be close in age, as many adult dogs don't appreciate the fumbling of inexperienced puppies. Consider the players' sizes as well. Some bigger puppies can self-handicap in order to play appropriately with smaller pups, but some overzealous pups don't understand their own size, and accidents can happen. For example, Olive used to enjoy playing with a neighbor boxer-mix puppy who was twelve weeks old, but when the puppy eclipsed her in size and didn't alter his play style to accommodate their differing heights and weights, Olive got testy with him. His rough and tumble play style was a little scary for her.

When selecting puppy play buddies, think about your puppy's play style as well. Some dogs like to wrestle, some like to chase, some like to be chased. Putting a wrestler with a chaser might not go well and make for a bad match. Remember, the goal is to tire out your dog in a constructive manner, not set her up to have hang-ups about being around other dogs.

It's easier than ever to find canine pals thanks to social media. Put out the call on Facebook or consider using Metup.com to find puppy buddies. Puppy friends can help to burn some of that boundless puppy energy and allow you to keep your home and your stuff in one piece!

Consider Doggie Day Care

If your puppy is climbing (and eating) the walls despite the bones, activity toys, walks, training, and games you're offering, think about enrolling her in a well-run day care. A day, or even a half day, of day care a few times a week can help to settle a restless canine spirit. The caveats in this suggestion are first making sure that your puppy enjoys the company of a group of other dogs, and then finding a center that offers *safe* play.

A well-run doggie day care will require that your puppy is at least four months of age and has been fully vaccinated. Your puppy should have to undergo an evaluation by the day-care staff to ensure that she is comfortable in the new environment and appropriate with other dogs. The facility should look, and more important, smell clean. The ratio of dogs to people should be at least one staffer to ten dogs. Ask if the staff receives any education in canine body language, and find out how dog-dog scuffles are defused. How are the dogs grouped? By age? By size? Do they stay on the indoor "playground" for the entire day, or do they get breaks to go outside? Where do they relieve themselves, and how is it cleaned up? Is there a rest period so that the dogs don't get overwhelmed from too much play? What is the protocol for injuries? Have there been any major dog fights with substantial injuries? Answers to these questions will help you assess if the facility is safe for your puppy.

If possible, watch your puppy for a while during her first visit to make sure that she's confident at the facility. Does she interact happily with the other dogs, or is she hiding in the corner? (Granted, some pups might need some time to assess the situation before committing to play.) Understand that not every puppy is a good fit for a day care, and that's completely fine! It doesn't mean that your puppy is abnormal; it just means your puppy wasn't comfortable in that environment.

Household Destruction and the Older Dog

Adult dogs that engage in household destruction might be suffering something more than just boredom or the need to chew. Although I believe separation anxiety is often misdiagnosed, there are many dogs that suffer from this debilitating disorder. The hallmarks of true S/A are self-injury in an attempt to escape confinement (like the dog that bloodies his nails trying to dig his way out of a crate), extreme vocalization, and household destruction, often near doorways. True separation anxiety usually requires the help of a veterinary behaviorist who can suggest behavioral modification exercises in conjunction with medication. Although we as a culture are primed to accept medication as the ultimate answer to behavioral problems, be aware that true progress is made when an owner works *with* her dog to achieve behavioral stability, instead of strictly relying on the medication to works its magic.

four

NIPPING AND BITING

Puppies explore the world with their mouths. Nipping and biting are acceptable communication within the dog world, but it's up to us to helps our pups understand that the rules are different with us humans. Although it seems like young puppies are part piranha, their nonstop mouthing is a completely normal developmental stage. It's critical to temper the biting through gentle dog-friendly methods that help the puppy understand that we have very delicate skin, and we don't like to be nipped.

Case Study: James and Kathleen rescued Dodger the spaniel-mix puppy as a Christmas gift for their twelve-year-old twin sons, Jackson and Taylor. The boys had wanted a dog for years, and the family had decided that everyone was finally ready to welcome a puppy into the household. Dodger was a typical puppy: curious, playful, and loving. He also had a nipping habit that drove the family crazy. Whenever the boys got down on the floor to play with him, Dodger leapt at them with his mouth wide open, biting frantically at their clothing and faces. James and the boys played rough with Dodger. They wrestled and tackled and laughed when the little dog came at them with his puppy fangs bared. When things got out of control and the nipping became unbearable, James and the boys clamped Dodger's muzzle shut. It didn't help curtail the nipping, it just made Dodger come back at them harder, but they kept it up because that's what their trainer told them would help.

Kathleen didn't like the way the boys played with the puppy because she thought it made him bite harder and more frequently. She tried to counterbalance the rough play by being extra gentle with Dodger. The problem was that when she tried to pet the dog, he would reach back and nip her hand every time. Kathleen worried that her five-month-old puppy was becoming aggressive, but her husband and sons wouldn't listen to her when she asked them to stop playing so rough.

Possible Outcome One: Dodger grew into a beautiful dog that never outgrew his nipping habit. When any of the boys played tug with Dodger, they were always guaranteed to receive at least one bruising nip on the hand as Dodger worked his way up the toy. When Dodger wanted to go out, or eat dinner, or get attention, he playfully nipped the rear end of the person standing closest to him. When offered a treat, Dodger clamped down painfully on the treat-giver's fingers, so the family always dropped the goodies on the floor to avoid contact with his rough mouth. Dodger faced the world with his piranha mouth open, and his human family members paid the price.

Possible Outcome Two: James bought a new big-screen TV and hired a professional to install it in his media room. The installer seemed wary of Dodger, so Kathleen made sure to keep the dog out of the room while he worked. The phone rang and Kathleen forgot to keep an eye on Dodger, who crept into the media room to watch what was going on. The installer's bag of supplies proved too tempting to resist, and Dodger grabbed a thick plastic-coated cable and started to gnaw on it a short distance away from the man. Annoyed, the installer walked over to where Dodger lay chewing and took the other end of the two-foot wire. Dodger leapt up and started tugging on the wire, and the installer placed his other hand on it in an attempt to yank it away. Dodger wasn't one to give up a game of tug easily, so he too worked his way up the wire growling playfully until his mouth was only inches from the man's hand. The man tugged roughly and in one balletic move, Dodger let go of the wire and reattached himself right on top of the installer's hands. Kathleen heard the man's startled cry from three rooms away. When she reached the room, she found the man holding his hands to his chest. Shaken, she asked to see them—thankfully there was no blood, just saliva and two indentations near his knuckle. She tried to convince him that everything was okay, and that Dodger had just been playing, but the man was so upset that he packed up his tools and raced out of the house. "I'm reporting that dog," the man said over his shoulder as he left. "Your dog bit me! I'm reporting him!"

Unchecked puppy mouthing can result in a lifetime of annoying and often painful nibbles, or can lead to major misunderstandings like the ones James and Kathleen experienced with the TV installer. Instead of curbing his mouthing when he was a puppy, they allowed, and even encouraged, their dog to use his mouth as a communicative device. How should they have handled Dodger's youthful nipping?

Early Mouthing Is a Necessary Step

Puppies bite, and it can get painful. The sooner we understand that it's a normal developmental stage and not aggression, the more quickly we can be prepared to deal with it properly. The truth is that we absolutely *must* allow puppies to mouth us when they're young. Gently mouthing hands and fingers is a critical step in the developmental process. It allows our pups to understand that we have delicate skin, and if they bite too hard we can get

Old-School Advice

You might have gotten advice about nipping that instructed you to clamp your puppy's mouth shut, as James and Kathleen did. Or perhaps you were told to flick your pup's nose, or "bop" him under the chin for nipping. While those tips might make *you* feel better (it's sort of like hitting a person who just hit you), they will do little to curb your puppy's nipping habit. Clamping the mouth shut usually makes the puppy bite even harder when released, and doesn't give her constructive feedback. (It can also make her hone her biting skills to become fast enough to avoid your hands.) Nose flicking and bopping are pain-based techniques, and why would you want to hurt your puppy for doing something that's a part of a normal developmental stage? Though the following "ouch" technique can be cumbersome, it's a dog-friendly, pain-free way to help your puppy understand that painful bites make the fun stop.

hurt, much the same way that their sibling pups did when they played too roughly with each other. If a puppy is never allowed contact with human skin, the pup never learns bite inhibition, or the ability to adjust the pressure of its mouth. An adult dog that never learned to control the force of its jaws as a puppy might react to getting stepped on accidentally by delivering a punishing bite, while the dog that learned to calibrate the force of its mouth might snap at the air near the offending foot, or, worst-case scenario, might place his mouth on it with no pressure. Bite inhibition is an important lesson that can literally save a dog's life.

Use the "Ouch!" Method

When puppies play together and one bites too roughly, the other pup will react with a shrill "yipe!" (When Olive and Millie play I often hear older sister Millie telling Olive to chill out by using a little shriek.) The biter usually takes it down a notch, and the play continues. If the biter forgets and continues to bite too roughly, the playmate often walks away from the game. We can use this same elegant technique to communicate the same message to our puppies.

You've probably noticed a difference in the ways your puppy chews on you. Sometimes it's with a soft mouth and it seems self-soothing, almost as if you're a pacifier for your puppy. Other times it's as if she's trying to perforate your entire body with her needle-teeth. The goal is to shape the mouthing from painful to pacifier, and then to nothing at all. When your

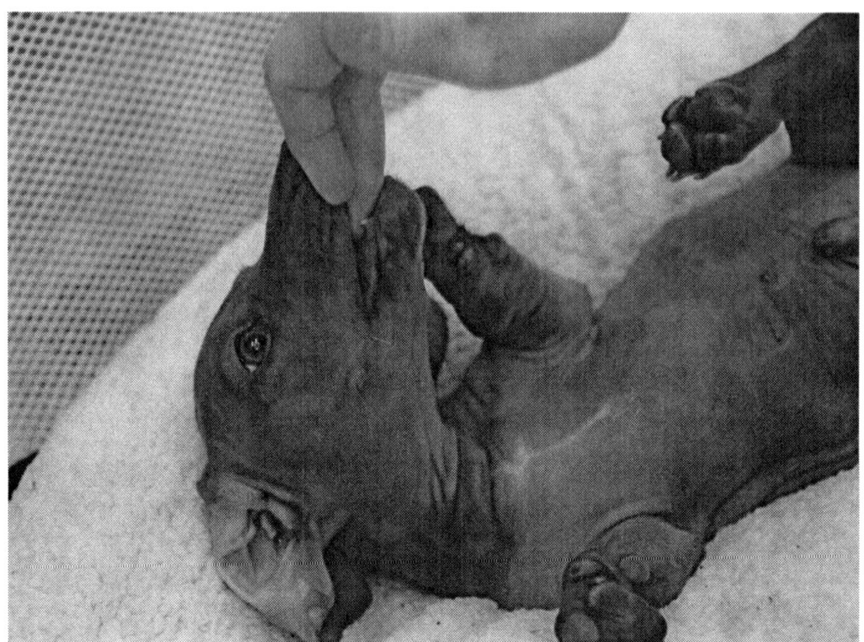

When puppy play tips over into crazy nipping, it's time to employ the "ouch" technique.

puppy is engaged in the gentle soft jaw mouthing, allow her to continue. When she escalates the mouthing and it begins to feel uncomfortable, say "ouch" loudly, remove your hands, and turn your body away from her for ten seconds. The word "ouch" is meant to mark the infraction—to let your puppy know what she did wrong—and removing your hand is brief time-out. Some trainers advise yipping like a puppy for too-hard bites, but I've found that many pups react to a high-pitch squeal by getting excited and biting more. A stage-worthy "ouch" is an effective-enough marker. Don't shout the word *at* your puppy as if you're yelling at her, as this can incite excitement as well. Say it to the wall across the room, with passion, as if your pup just removed your finger.

My clients often tell me that they've tried the "ouch" technique and it doesn't work for them, since they say it and it only stops their pup from nipping for a few seconds. The secret to employing this method effectively, however, is in the next step: social isolation. If your puppy comes back at you with the same level of intensity, repeat the dramatic "ouch" again, but this time get up and walk away from your puppy. Social isolation is one of the most powerful punishments for a puppy, as they want nothing more than to be with their people. If your timing is good, your puppy will soon understand that when she bites too hard, her person goes away. I employ a "two strikes, you're out"" rule with very young puppies instead of getting

Learning about Nipping

Puppies that leave their mother and littermates before they reach eight weeks are often handicapped in the bite inhibition department. The lessons learned about nipping from fellow dogs between six and eight weeks of age are incredibly important. Puppies that miss this stage might end up biting more often and harder than puppies that stay with their littermates, so don't bring home a pup until she's more than eight weeks old. (In some states it's illegal to bring home a pup under eight weeks of age, anyway.)

up the very first time they bite too hard. As the pup matures and starts to understand what "ouch" means, I give them only one shot to get it right. If your puppy is particularly revved up and continues chomping down even after the "ouch," put her in her crate for a brief rest. (This isn't a punishment, it's merely a time-out.)

Once your puppy has stopped delivering hard nips and uses only a soft mouth on you when you interact, pretend as if even the soft bites hurt. When her mouth lands on your hand, say, "Ouch!" and walk away as you've been doing for the hard bites. After fine-tuning her bite inhibition, your puppy will understand that she shouldn't put her mouth on your skin, but if she has to (like the startled dog that was accidentally stepped on), she'll calibrate accordingly.

Hand Feed Meals

Encouraging your pup to eat her meals from your hands has many benefits. First, it helps her to understand that your hands bring good things, specifically food! Take a handful of your puppy's meal and put it in your cupped hand, but don't allow your puppy to be pushy and dive in before you're ready. This is an excellent opportunity to teach your pup some basic manners. Move your hands away from your puppy and ask her to sit, and the second her bum hits the ground, open your hands and allow her to eat. (She doesn't have to hold the sit for longer than a second initially—you can work up to making her hold it for longer periods during future meals.) Allow your puppy to eat as long as she maintains a gentle mouth. If she slips up and pinches your skin with her teeth, say "ouch!" and remove your hands for a few seconds, and then offer your cupped hands again.

In addition to encouraging a soft mouth, hand feeding also teaches your pup that people near her food means good things. Rather than feeling the

Feeding your puppy his meals from your hand can help to build a soft mouth.

need to guard her food from people, the hand-fed puppy will welcome them.

Offer Chewable Substitutions

One of the easiest ways to redirect a nipping puppy is to offer her a suitable substitution, like a bone or treat-stuffed activity toy. This means that you should have a variety of them planted around the house, so if your puppy decides to start grabbing your robe while you're brushing your teeth in the bathroom, you have something nearby to give her. Though it's tempting to buy only one or two chew bones or toys, variety is imperative during the teething phase. (And I say this as a dog trainer, not a dog supply store owner.) Not only do dogs get bored of the same old same old, but you should also have enough suitable options so that you can have one in every room.

My favorite bones for puppies are bully sticks and hollow marrow bones. The bully sticks are tasty enough to coax even the most hyperactive puppy into a calm chewing trance. Marrow bones work well because you can restuff them with peanut butter or any of the stuffers listed on page 45. A great treat-stuffable toy option for a crazy nippy puppy is one that requires the pup to work actively to get the treat. Some treat toys are great for crate time because they don't require the pup to move around to dispense the goodies, but when you're dealing with a puppy that has the biting zoomies, you want a toy that forces her to get up and go to get the goodies out.

Work on Gentle Treat Taking

Olive is crazy about food, and her food drive made it difficult to give her treats without nearly losing skin, so I worked on softening up her mouth in a couple of different ways.

- **The spoon technique**: Instead of giving Olive a treat directly from my fingers, I took a spoon and cradled the treat in the middle of it using my thumb. (I held the spoon near her bowl rather than at the end of the utensil.) I then turned the spoon sideways so that when she went to grab the treat, she felt a little bit of my thumb but more of the unyielding metal. It's an easy way to keep your skin in the game (literally) while at the same time using the slight aversive of the metal to keep the puppy from clamping down.
- **The fist technique:** For this technique I put the treat in my fist and offered it to Olive. In her excitement to get to it she clamped down on my fist. (It's not nearly as painful as a bite to the fingers!) I waited until Olive backed off and stopped biting, and then I opened my fist

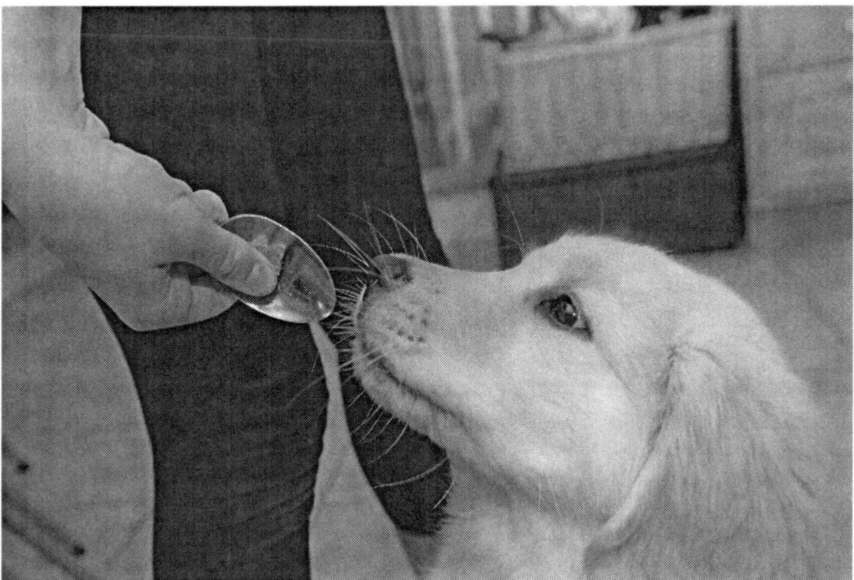

The spoon technique can transform a piranha puppy into a gentle treat taker.

and presented the treat. Her initial reaction to the fist was almost always "*CHOM* . . . lick . . . step back and wait." In time your puppy will understand that the only way you'll open your fist is to refrain from using a hard mouth.

Play Happens Only with Toys

James and his sons played hands-on and rough with Dodger. Their wrestling blurred the lines of acceptable behavior with their dog, which contributed to Dodger retaining his rough mouth well past puppyhood. To help underscore the idea that teeth don't belong on skin, particularly when the puppy gets excited, play should happen only with a toy in between person and dog.

Although it's fun to get down on the ground and rile up a puppy, it can confuse her about what type of behavior is permitted. Kathleen didn't like rough play, but when she tried to interact with Dodger, he came at her with the same level of intensity he used when playing with her boys. The family's scenario was doubly challenging because the young sons also played rough with Dodger. They couldn't always fend him off when he came at them with his teeth bared, which resulted in punctures, bruising, and hard feelings.

Making sure that play happens only with a toy can help teach a puppy that grabbing on to hands and ankles during play isn't permitted. If you're playing tug (with rules described on pages 51–53) and your puppy works his way up the toy and onto your hand, shriek "ouch" to mark the behavior, and then drop the toy and walk away. If you're playing fetch and your puppy tries to grab the ball from your hand, drop the ball and walk away. I often hear people say, "Oh, my puppy didn't mean to nip me! He was going for the toy!" Despite their clumsy carriage, puppies have an amazing ability to hone their mouths' trajectory, so don't write off all of those playtime nips to misfires.

There are some games that don't require a toy, as outlined in my book *Bonding with Your Dog.* Hide-and-seek and tricks training, for example, are wonderful ways to burn energy and build the bond. Like any appropriate game, they require rules and polite behavior from all parties.

Acknowledge "Please-Don't-Pet-Me" Nips

It's a little heartbreaking when we attempt to pet our adorable puppy and our kindness is met by a bite, particularly when it seems to happen *every*

The Pants Police

Many puppies can't resist latching on to flappy pant legs or shoelaces. Unfortunately, this usually happens in the morning when you're wearing pajamas, and the last thing you feel like doing is training your dog. Puppies love a moving target and things that "play back," and trying to kick your puppy off your clothing will do nothing but make her more likely to latch tighter. In dog training, if a behavior is predictable, it's preventable. If you *know* that your puppy loves to chase pajamas, or your evening sweatpants, or your daughter's fuzzy slippers, prepare for the inevitable. Set up a tether (a leash secured to a heavy piece of furniture), grab a handful of treats, roll your pants up to avoid tempting her before you're ready, and put your puppy on the tether. Then roll your pants down again and walk past your pup very slowly so that your movements don't incite the chase. The goal is to capture your puppy *refraining* from chasing your pants, so if you can pass without your pup lunging for you, mark the behavior by saying "good!" and toss her a treat. Walk past again, and mark the lack of lunging by saying "good" and tossing another treat. Work up to walking by quickly and with some "swish" while your puppy waits politely for her treat. Get your children involved as well if their clothing is also targeted, but assist them with the treat delivery to ensure proper timing. You can use a tether if your puppy gets too excited and nippy when you play with her as well. That way you can walk away from her and she can't chase along behind you, biting your ankles or your rear end.

If your puppy decides that your plain old jeans are good enough to herd and you're not prepared to do tether training, stop moving instead of trying to fight her off. Some puppies give up and let go when the target gets boring, at which time you should give her a treat and lots of praise, then redirect her to a toy or bone. If your puppy doesn't let go, use the "drop it" cue as described on page 44, and instead of giving the treat directly to your puppy, toss it a few steps away so she has to move in order to get it. This will prevent her from taking the treat and grabbing on again. Curbing a pants addiction doesn't take a great deal of effort, but it does require that you prepare for the attack!

time we try to pet. Don't all dogs love to be touched? Most do, but many pass through a stage during puppyhood when they seem like they don't enjoy petting at all. It's important to recognize it and respond appropriately.

If you pet your puppy and you get a nip in response, back off for a moment. I understand that it feels like the divine right of puppy ownership to pet your puppy when you feel like it, but continuing to try to pet when she's in piranha mode will only frustrate both of you. Now, I'm not referring to chronically hand-shy puppies. There's a difference between the puppy that consistently backs away from handling and the one that gets nippy when she doesn't feel like being touched because she's overstimulated and punchy. (You can use the "touch-for-a-treat" technique mentioned in the opening of this book to help puppies that don't tolerate any sort of handling.) Rather than force the issue and try to pet your puppy against her will, just take a break from the petting for a day. Interact with her through constructive play, and let her initiate touch once she calms down. Rest assured, the "don't-pet-me" stage is a fleeting part of puppyhood, and you'll get your cuddly best friend back in no time!

Nipping and the Adult Dog

Dealing with an adult nipper takes Teflon fingers and a tender heart. The adult dog that still takes treats with a rough mouth or still bites for attention needs to learn immediately that communication with teeth is unacceptable. The good news is that the adult dog that bites gently is demonstrating respectable bite inhibition. The dog understands not to clamp down and break skin, but she hasn't learned to resist the urge to "talk with her teeth."

These adult biters might have come from a home like James and Kathleen's, where puppy nipping was never weaned down, or they might come from a rescue situation where they didn't have the opportunity to interact properly with people during the critical bite inhibition stage. (In this scenario I'm specifically referring to adult dogs that nip during play or for attention, not those that bite defensively, like when they're being pulled out from under the bed or being otherwise handled.)

The same rules apply to adult piranha dogs as to puppies, but the stakes are higher. A nip from an underdeveloped puppy jaw is usually far less painful than one from a fully grown dog!

Use the "ouch" technique: The exact same technique you use to help a puppy understand how delicate we are can be used with the adult nipper as well. I employ a "one-strike-you're-out" rule with adult nippers. The first time a tooth strays onto skin, shout "ouch" and get up and walk away. Leave the room if necessary, wait thirty seconds, and then come back in as if nothing happened. Continue to mark the nips, but if the process devolves into a nonstop stream of "ouch and go," take a break for a while.

How Can You Tell If Your Dog Is Communicating Discomfort?

Although it sometimes seems like a dog gives no indication as to how he's feeling and then lashes out without warning, it's more likely that the dog has given signals that are either too subtle to see without specifically looking for them, or the observer doesn't understand how to read the dog's display. In the case of resource guarding, the dog might freeze and hover over her bowl. She might keep her body still but rotate her eye so that it's facing the direction of the perceived threat, so that the whites of her eye show. She might begin to consume her food at a faster rate than before the threat approached. And the most obvious indicator of discomfort: she might growl and snap directly at the person or animal approaching her bowl. Avoid punishing a dog displaying these types of signals. The dog is providing you with important feedback—"I want you to know that this makes me uncomfortable!"—and punishing the dog for it will merely suppress the reaction, not change the reason behind it. Then, when a lesser-perceived threat approaches, like a child, the dog might react with a greater level of intensity. Dogs are always communicating; it's up to us to learn to read what they're saying.

Hand feed: Hand feeding an adult dog first requires ensuring the dog has no resource-guarding issues, meaning the dog is already comfortable having you near his food bowl. If your dog is reactive when you or anyone in your family gets too close to his food, get help from a trainer to work on resource-guarding issues before you dive into hand feeding.

The same rules for puppy hand feeding apply for adult hand feeding as well. Don't allow your dog to be pushy and take food from your hand before you're ready, and make her do a "sit" or "down" before you begin the process. Allow your dog to continue eating as long as she's able to keep from nipping your skin.

Play with toys: Although some trainers don't agree with me, I believe that hand-to-hand combat like wrestling is an unacceptable way to interact with your dog, particularly with a dog that has nipping issues. For that reason, play should involve a toy. Misfires, which occur when your dog "accidentally" latches on to your hand or body, should be met with an "ouch" and a brief cessation of the game. Take the toy and walk away with it, ignoring your dog. If she jumps up and tries to nip or grab at the toy, go somewhere where she can't reach you. More than three misfires during playtime means game over. An adult dog should be able to take breaks during play to perform a quick "sit" or "down," which will keep the game polite and under control.

Provide suitable substitutions: Like their younger counterparts, many adult dogs like to chew on bones and activity toys, too! Just because a dog has moved out of the teething phase doesn't mean that he no longer has a need or desire to chew. Our boxer, Sumner, chewed on bones until he was more than ten years old. Finding what your dog loves to chew will keep him constructively occupied with something other than your fingers.

Work on gentle treat taking: You can use the exact same techniques as you did with puppies to help your adult hard-mouthed dog to gently take treats from your hand. (I meet many adult dogs with hard mouths in my store, and it surprises me that their people just tolerate it instead of working to change it!) The fist technique or the spoon technique detailed on page 63 can help drive home the point that no matter how excited your dog is to get a treat, he must do it with a gentle mouth.

It Gets Better

It might feel like your puppy is abnormal and aggressive when the nipping gets intense, but rest assured, it's a typical part of the maturation process. Some forethought, planning, and patience—the ingredients for success in all things dog—will help to ease this often painful stage of puppyhood. Addressing mouthing and nipping calmly and with puppy-friendly techniques should make it stop before your bruises fade and the punctures on your hands heal!

five

JUMPING UP

When a sweet, tiny puppy jumps up to say hello, it's nearly impossible not to lean down and acknowledge it with a smile and a pat. A small puppy jumping up doesn't seem like it could be a problem, but from a developmental standpoint, turning that leap into a mindful interaction can shed some light as to what's just down the road. An eight-week-old puppy, no matter what breed, probably doesn't weigh enough to do any damage or cause any pain. But take a moment to forecast what will happen if the jumping continues as the dog matures. In just a matter of weeks, the larger-breed puppies may begin inflicting discomfort when they jump, and even the smaller jumpers can become a nuisance without causing pain. Jumping up is one of my pet peeves, and even though I have worked to avoid it with Olive and Millie since they were young, a series of well-intentioned visitors in my store have taught them that jumping up is a good thing, much like the couple in our case study.

Case Study: Allison and her fiancé, Chet, considered Gus the yellow lab puppy their "practice baby" before they started working on the real thing. They owned a small interior design store, so they were able to bring Gus to work with them from the day he came home, where he joyfully greeted everyone from the delivery man to their most important clients, showing his affection by hopping up and licking hands. The puppy was literally a traffic stopper; he liked to hang out in front of the window of their street-level location, and people would tap on the glass and laugh when he danced on the other side.

Allison was pleased with the nonstop socialization Gus received in and around the office. No one could resist the adorable ten-week-old puppy. His jumping up was always met with pats and cuddles, and sometimes people even picked him up. Chet occasionally tried to get people to stop petting Gus when he was jumping, but his clients and friends always told him, "It's okay if he jumps, I love dogs!"

Gus grew quickly. His puppy tubbiness disappeared, and his adorable waddling leaps of greeting started to land higher and higher on the objects of his affection. The delivery man that used to love to pet Gus started lowering the boxes he was delivering in front of his legs so that Gus couldn't scratch him when he greeted him. Allison and Chet took to scolding him, saying over and over, "Gus, get down. Get down!" when he jumped on anyone, because at six months old, the puppy was starting to hurt people. Not only was his jumping up for attention painful, but it was also embarrassing. For example, when the couple had welcomed a new high-profile client to their office, Gus leaped on her so passionately that he got dirt on her dress and put a runner in her stockings. Over the span of a few months, their sweet puppy changed from a furry welcoming committee to a leaping menace that visitors tried to avoid.

***Possible Outcome One*:** Allison mentions Gus's jumping to their veterinarian during a routine checkup. He tells her that the best way to deal with it is to knee the dog in the chest when he jumps, to "be the alpha." The vet goes on to tell her that Gus is jumping on them to show his dominance, and if they don't stop the behavior, Gus is likely to spiral out of control. Allison is so concerned about raising a bad dog that she takes her vet's advice to heart. When Gus jumps on her, she raises her knee to hit him in the chest, but Gus tolerates each blow like a professional hockey player. He finds a way to jump on her so that she can't get her knee up quickly enough, and she ends up looking like she and the dog are doing an uncomfortable dance together. Chet doesn't have the heart to knee Gus, so he continues to tell the dog to "stop-stop-stop" like a broken record, and gently removes his paws from his chest. Allison instructs visitors to their studio to try to knee Gus, but no one feels comfortable with the maneuver. No matter how hard he gets hit, even if he falls backwards onto the ground, Gus always comes back for more.

Possible Outcome Two: Chet and Allison realize that Gus's jumping is becoming a problem when the delivery guy starts leaving their packages outside the door for them instead of coming in. They attend a training class with Gus, and he excels at everything, but he just won't listen to them when they tell him to sit for greeting. His jumping remains out of control even though they chant "Sit! Gus, sit! Sit!" and place dry biscuits in front of his nose. When they have important clients visiting the studio, they lock Gus in a conference room and then have to listen to him howl while they hold their meeting.

Uncontrollable jumping is such a typical problem that it's almost a guarantee for certain breeds. The early reinforcement we offer by acknowledging and petting jumping dogs during puppyhood coupled with the feel-good factor the dog experiences when he leaps makes for a daunting untraining process. It's difficult to rewire a jumper, but it's not impossible. Here's how.

Ignore Jumping Up

The number-one secret to avoiding a lifetime of jumping up is to never, ever, *ever* acknowledge your puppy when she does it. It's such a simple bit of advice, but it's *so* difficult to enforce! It feels heartless to ignore the tiny baby puppy that jumps up looking for cuddles. The problem, as illustrated by what happened with Gus and his people, is that the behavior takes over like a kudzu vine. Dogs do what works, and if jumping up works to get your attention—even if it's angry attention—your puppy will continue to do it. Once you've cemented this pattern, your puppy will jump, because all she's trying to do is to get you to notice her.

If you have a brand-new puppy and family and friends willing to help out, you'll probably be able to avoid the pox that is the jumpy dog. Ignoring jumps for attention is yet another example of where mindful interactions will serve you well. Instead of absentmindedly stroking your puppy while she plants her paws on your leg, step aside so that she can't. When she slides off into a standing position, or better yet, a sit, praise until you go hoarse, and pet until your hand falls off! *Always* be mindful when interacting your puppy, and ask yourself, "Do I like this behavior? Do I want it to continue?" Requesting that your family and close friends to do the same will ensure that your puppy is never inadvertently reinforced for jumping up. I'll repeat it: ignoring your dog is not easy. I can't tell you how many times I caught my husband petting Olive while she tried to scale his leg. And even more challenging, a puppy jump doesn't always feel like a jump, particularly when you're dealing with a petite dog. Sometimes it's a subtle reach up that you can barely even feel. Sometimes it happens when you bend down to pet your puppy—when you're consciously trying to prevent jumping! Any time those front paws come up off the ground and you acknowledge it, your puppy is getting feedback from you. You're basically telling your puppy, "This *works,* little one!"

Jumping up is cute when dogs are little, but it can quickly become a tiresome habit.

The task gets more challenging when you step outside your front

Is Jumping Up a Power Play?

Old-school vets and trainers say that jumping up is an indicator of a dog exhibiting dominance. This perspective is dangerous to maintaining a healthy bond with your dog, as it recasts what is a natural exuberant expression into a power play. Jumping greetings aren't our dogs' attempts to "dominate" us. It's an attention-seeking behavior that typically develops in puppyhood—"Notice me! Pet me!"—that is accidentally nurtured with attention (even angry attention!) and then difficult to extinguish. Dominance? Not even close.

door and your puppy is faced with dozens of admiring strangers. Chet and Allison didn't realize that allowing their clients to pet puppy Gus when he was jumping up would set a precedent that seemed nearly impossible to fix. It's not easy to be the puppy police when someone wants to interact with your dog, but it's critical that everyone follows the same protocol. I've lived through this issue with Olive in my store, and I've accidentally offended dozens of people by trying to engineer proper greetings! I desperately wanted Olive to be a "four-paws-on-the-floor" kind of greeter since I knew that she was going to be spending a lot of time with me at the store. Whenever someone came in I'd ask, "Please don't pet her if she jumps up, we're in training!" Now, *I* thought I was being pleasant, but more than a few shoppers seemed put off by my request. "Oh, you have a *strict* mommy, don't you, puppy?" I'd hear them say as Olive planted her paws on their shins. Others would answer like Chet and Allison's customers: "It's okay if she jumps, I love puppies! She's soooo cute!" If my requests to ignore jumping fell on deaf ears, I'd walk out from behind the counter with a treat and call Olive back to my side while I gently tried to explain why I was teaching her not to jump. Unfortunately, people didn't want to hear it. Olive's intermittent schedule of reinforcement proved to be a very effective way to teach her to jump on everyone that walked into my store. Eventually, Olive grew from a six-pound mass of white curls to a thirty-pound knee-bruiser with a robust jumping habit.

I have been diligent about working on the behavior despite the setbacks, and Olive is making steady improvement. Millie, on the other hand, remains an unrepentant but gentle jumper. She's a wispy fourteen pounds of canine adorableness, so no matter how much I plead with people to refrain from petting her when she's jumping up, they just don't listen. Of the two, Millie's gentle jumps are preferable to Olive's crazed hip-grazing leaps.

Just Whistle

It's not easy to deal with my dogs jumping up on people in my store, because I'm often helping someone at the counter when other people walk in and get jumped on. Since I can't be in two places at once, I devised a simple work-around solution that has put a dent in their impolite jumping. Both dogs alert to the sound of the door opening. They then typically race to whomever is entering and stand at their feet for a few seconds. (For some reason the jumping up is a delayed reaction.) Instead of letting the dogs remain near the person until he or she looks down and acknowledges them (which is their cue to jump up), I blow a soft but high-pitched dog whistle. I've trained them to understand that every time they hear the whistle, they're to come running back to me for a treat. The whistle is an incredibly powerful cue for them, and it's rare that they ignore it to continue interacting with the person. After they come to me to collect their treats, the "greet-then-jump" behavioral chain is short-circuited, and they can mill around with the person without feeling the need to jump up. Of course, I can't always blow the whistle in time, but I've found that it's an easy work-around to this challenging problem.

Ignoring the jumping up is only half of the equation. In positive dog training, we preach that you should ignore what you don't like and acknowledge what you do. In the jumping-up scenario, it's critical to acknowledge your puppy any time she opts to keep four on the floor when greeting you, or better yet, if she sits for greeting. I can't stress it enough: it's a huge, wonderful gift when your puppy starts to understand that jumping doesn't work and offers you a sit or a stand instead. Even if you want your puppy to ultimately sit for greeting and she's only offering you four paws on the floor, take it! Standing instead of jumping is a foundation behavior that can easily turn into a sit down the road. Don't just look for the finished product—always acknowledge baby steps in the right direction.

The word "acknowledge" is open to interpretation, of course. When praising a puppy for keeping four on the floor, try to keep your voice at a pitch that doesn't encourage celebratory jumping. I've watched Olive execute a perfect stand for greeting only to have a well-intentioned shopper bend over and praise her in a way that incited a "Thanks-for-noticing my-good-manners" leap after the fact. I'm keenly aware of how my voice and praising style affects my dogs' reactions. When I arrive home, I quietly say, almost in a whisper, "Good girls are *good* girls!" to them. My low-key acknowledgment of them helps them to refrain from spastic jumping.

"Acknowledge" can also mean treats, of course. Giving your puppy a treat for standing or sitting instead of jumping will certainly drive the point home more quickly! The means of treat delivery is important. Hand over the treat when your puppy is doing anything but jumping. You can click to precisely mark your puppy's body position and then follow up with a treat. Delivering a treat to a small dog can be cumbersome, as you have to make sure that your puppy maintains four paws on the floor even when she's taking the treat. That means bending over instead of letting her dance on her back legs to collect her payment. (In fact, encourage your puppy to keep four paws on the floor as much as possible. As a rule, nothing good happens when those front paws lift off the ground!)

Teach the "Arm-Cross Sit"

As noted in the previous section, one of the biggest challenges of teaching a puppy not to jump up is dealing with the human side of the equation. We all adore puppies! Well-intentioned but inappropriate acknowledgment of jumpy greetings sets the stage for a lifetime of leaping, so it's important to gently instruct would-be petters about proper greeting etiquette. Instead of telling people what *not* to do, it's easier—and more friendly—to tell them what they *can* do instead.

When puppies are excited, it's almost as if their ears fuse shut. You could tell a puppy to "sit" a dozen times, but if she's more interested in meeting an adoring fan, she's not going to listen. Dogs are always keyed in to our body language, which makes the following arm-cross exercise a very effective way of dealing with jumping. Not only does it show the puppy what she needs to do, it also provides very clear direction as to what the person should do to greet properly. Instead of accidentally encouraging jumping up with body language or tone of voice, new friends will understand that they need to get a sit before they can interact with the puppy.

To begin, grab a handful of treats and take your puppy to a quiet room. Walk a few paces and then come to a stop facing your puppy. Cross your arms across your chest, and wait for your puppy to collapse into a sit. (Don't ask your puppy to sit, just wait; we want this to be a purely nonverbal cue.) Ignore any leaps for attention. Look away and step off to the side if your puppy jumps on you, keeping in mind that *any* attention, even a glance in her direction, might keep the jumping going. The second your puppy sits (and it will happen), click or acknowledge the behavior with a verbal marker like "yup!" or "good" and then hand over the treat. Move a few steps away and repeat the process: come to a stop, cross your arms, and wait for the sit. Reward it and repeat until your puppy is reliably

The arm-cross sit is an easy fix for jumpy dogs of all sizes.

offering a sit every time she sees you cross your arms. Enlist everyone in your household to do the same, so that your puppy understands that crossed arms are a cue to sit. (Of course, you should also teach your puppy a verbal sit cue during other training sessions.)

Work on the behavior near the door or doors that visitors normally enter. Practice knocking on the door or ringing the doorbell, coming inside, and doing the arm-cross sit. Ask friends and neighbors to come over and do the same, so that soon your puppy will understand that even if she's meeting a new person, crossed arms means that she should sit.

I've found that compliance on the human side of the equation is all about how you ask. People are likely to be more responsive if you say, "Hey, my puppy knows a really cool trick so that she won't jump up on you. All you have to do is cross your arms like this and she'll sit!" Even though it's a great idea to let strangers feed your puppy treats, when you're working on jumping up, it's usually best if you do the treat delivery post-sit. Many well-intentioned people hold the treat in the air so that the puppy has to jump up to get it, which negates the very exercise she performed in order to earn the treat! The arm-cross sit is helpful for children as well. Kids tend to get over-excited when meeting a puppy, which can elicit jumping up. Showing them how to do the arm-cross sit allows them to interact with the puppy in a constructive fashion.

The arm-cross sit is a simple way to help prevent jumping up from taking root. It's a helpful cue that happens to be pretty darn cool as well!

Remedial Jumping-Up Training

Ignoring jumping up is a great strategy for tiny puppies, but it's a less-than-helpful tip when the jumper is a sixty-five-pound adult dog. It takes a great deal of resolve to ignore that kind of greeting, along with a willingness to get bruised and scratched in the process! Jumpy greetings are normally cemented during puppyhood, so what do you do if you missed the boat and your dog has been jumping up for ages? Or what if you adopted an adult dog that has an entrenched jumping habit?

It's never too late to begin remedial work, but I must caution you that this is one of the more challenging nuisance behaviors to work on. (This is why I keep harping on early prevention!) It's deeply reinforcing for dogs to jump because it feels good to expend built-up energy and leap up and touch you, and because they typically get rewarded during the interaction. Even if you think that yelling at your dog to stop or kneeing him in the chest is an effective inhibitor, to your dog it's probably an invitation to the party! (Ask yourself if those techniques worked for you. If not, it's time to rethink your strategy.)

Jumping-up training is contextual. Although it would be wonderful if your dog could generalize the training that you do in a classroom to every situation in which he meets exciting new people, it doesn't usually happen that way. For that reason, let's take a look at how to train your dog not to jump up in the three most common jumpy scenarios: greeting you when you come home, greeting your guests when they visit, and greeting strangers out in the world.

Greeting you at home: This is a low-pressure training scenario, meaning you can anticipate the intensity of your dog's jumping and plan accordingly since you've been living with it for a while. Before you enter the house, prepare by grabbing a handful of super-high-value treats. (Dry boring biscuits aren't going to cut it for this one.) Walk in and remain calm, even if you're thrilled to see your dog and want to give her a great big hug. She will probably come barreling at you, and instead of greeting her head-on as you normally do, turn your back to her and ignore her. Unfortunately, you will get jumped on, perhaps more than usual since you're not interacting with dog. Don't look at her or touch her while she's jumping. Believe it or not, there will come a moment when your dog stops jumping and just stands still. It might be fleeting, but it *will* happen. Acknowledge the lack of jumping—the standing—with a click or a marker word like "yup," and toss the treat a few steps away from your dog so that she has to walk away from you to get it. (It might help to quickly place the treat in front of your dog's nose and then toss it. Many dogs lose their treat-tracking abilities when they're overstimulated.) Tossing the treat is like hitting the reset button: it gives you a chance to take a breath and prepare and allows your dog to blow off a little excess energy by tracking down the treat.

Your dog will probably approach and launch herself at you after she's eaten the treat. Turn away and stand still, once again waiting for your dog to stop jumping. Mark that happy moment with a click or "yup," and toss the treat again. You can attempt to pet your dog while she's standing and not jumping, but be forewarned that your touch might send her into the stratosphere and trigger more jumping! Repeat a few times until your dog starts to understand that she gets petting and a treat for keeping four paws on the floor. When your dog is slightly calmer, make her work harder by waiting for her to offer you a sit. (Dogs usually figure out pretty quickly that if treats are present, sitting almost guarantees getting one.) It's actually easier to initially capture your dog standing instead of jumping than it is to try to get a sit. Every dog is going to stop jumping and stand eventually, which means that you can start rewarding your dog more quickly for standing instead of waiting for a perfect sit. You can then build a sit from the calm standing position. Of course, you can use the arm-cross sit technique to make the process even easier. Simply greet your dog with crossed arms, wait for the sit, and then toss the treat as described above.

In my household, Millie and Olive usually do well with their initial greeting, even though they are beyond excited to greet their people. They've figured out that they need to keep four paws on the ground when I first enter, but they had a hard time resisting jumping on me when I started to walk toward the back door to let them out. To combat this, I used my verbal marker "yup" to capture them for trotting along beside me without jumping up. So when I first walk in the door and see them, I wait for a sit and then toss each dog a treat. I give them a few pats and then we start walking to the door. If Millie manages to walk beside me without jumping I say, "Yup Millie!" and toss the treat a few steps in front of her. Olive usually notices the treat delivery and stops jumping in order to get one as well. Our walk to the door is very calm, with both dogs in competition to see who can get the most treats for being good. It would be easy to wean them from the treats over time, but it's such a simple way to acknowledge what I know is very challenging behavior for them.

Greeting visitors to your home: Jump training gets a little more difficult when you add the sound of the doorbell and new faces. The foyer can be a very stimulating spot for a dog. It's the only place in the house where things like strange men with packages, pizza, and friends magically appear! Add to that the fact that many people accidentally encourage jumpy greetings, which serves to undo any of the hard work you've done. Unfortunately, putting your dog away in another room when guests arrive only delays the jumpy reaction. It's a fine way to get people into the house without being immediately accosted (which is helpful if someone is bringing a small child or if someone is unstable on their feet), but once you release your dog, the typical leaping will ensue. Dealing with jumpy greeting is a challenge because you want to be able to focus on the person visiting you, not worry about training your dog. Couple that with the fact that your dog's reactions are probably embarrassing, and that makes for a stressful situation.

The training technique for greeting guests takes out of the equation the full-body contact that *you* had to deal with during training. Instead of allowing your dog to jump up on your guests, use a short tether to keep her close enough to the action so that she can learn the rules, but not so close that she can put her paws on anyone. A tether is a short leash (preferably less than four feet) that is secured to a stable piece of furniture near your front door so that your dog should have a clear view of anyone coming in. Before you begin practicing with real human victims on the other side of your front door, get your dog excited about going to the tether. Some dogs quickly figure out that the tether means a temporary loss of freedom, and they resist going near it, which turns the first step of the training process into a "catch-me-if-you-can" game.

To help your dog acclimate, bring her to the tether spot, attach her to it, and feed her a few savory goodies. Try to use a novel treat. Repeat the process a few times (you can even use a casual teach-as-you-go cue like "tether up!") so that your dog understands that good things happen when she's on the tether. Then make it more difficult for her: ring the doorbell or knock on the door and then put her on the tether. It doesn't matter if your dog sees you ringing or knocking—the reaction will be just as dramatic as if it's a real visitor on the other side of the door. "Tethering up" won't be quite as easy after you've introduced this bit of reality to the process! Repeat the ringing/knocking process a few more times, always making sure to give your dog a treat when she's on the tether. You want her to begin to make the connection that when she hears someone at the door, she needs to go on the tether. When you're done training, release her from it without fanfare. It helps to leave the tether in place so you don't have to hunt for it when you need it.

Now you're ready to attempt the process with stunt visitors! Ask a kind neighbor to knock on your door, and then put your dog on the tether as practiced. Welcome your faux guest in and interact with her as you would with any real guest. By now, your dog will probably be leaping at the end of the tether, eager to show the guest her own warm welcome. Do not move toward your dog when she's jumping. The moment she has four paws on the floor, walk with your guest toward her. If she begins jumping again, turn your backs and ignore her. When she settles again, continue moving toward her. This is an "attract/repel" training scenario. When your dog is calm and stands instead of jumping, she attracts you to come closer to her. If she jumps up and acts out of control, she repels you and you turn away from her. When your guest is just outside of the "strike zone"—where your dog is close but can't quite reach the person—ask the person to cross her arms as described on pages 74–75. If you've been practicing, your dog *should* go into a sit, and you can reward her by tossing that super-special treat a few steps away from where she is standing. When she comes back, do the arm-cross sit again and toss the treat. Repeat a few more times until your dog has figured out the game. Ask your guest to interact with your dog, keeping in mind that petting might make her jump up again. If she does, you and your guest should step beyond the reach of the tether until she has calmed. When your dog has made successful contact with your guest, give her a special treat-stuffed activity toy and send her on her way.

Unfortunately, jumpy front-door greeting behavior does not go away quickly. It takes determination and a great deal of practice to put a dent in it because the behavior is usually deeply rewarding for the dog. Couple that fact with friendly strangers who love your dog no matter what she's doing, and you've got an entrenched behavior. There's no such thing as working on this behavior too much. Your antijump friends (count me as one of them!) will thank you for doing so.

Greeting strangers in the real world: A stranger's willingness to help train your dog in the real world is highly variable. Some people are more than happy to pitch in for a few minutes, while others just want to pet your dog and don't care if they get jumped on. Because your dog is on a leash when out in the real world, you have a modicum of control. Most six-foot leashes (or worse yet, extendable leashes), however, allow your dog ample space to leap on new friends while you stand helpless on the other end. In addition, you might ask the stranger to assist you only to get the standard "It's okay if she jumps on me," even though you've already stated that you're working on stopping the behavior!

There is a quick and easy way to gain more control when your dog meets a stranger: become an anchor on the leash by standing on it at the midpoint. (This technique doesn't work well with flexible leashes, as the thin cord can slip out from under your foot.) Before the person is within your dog's strike zone, meaning before your dog can reach out and touch the person,

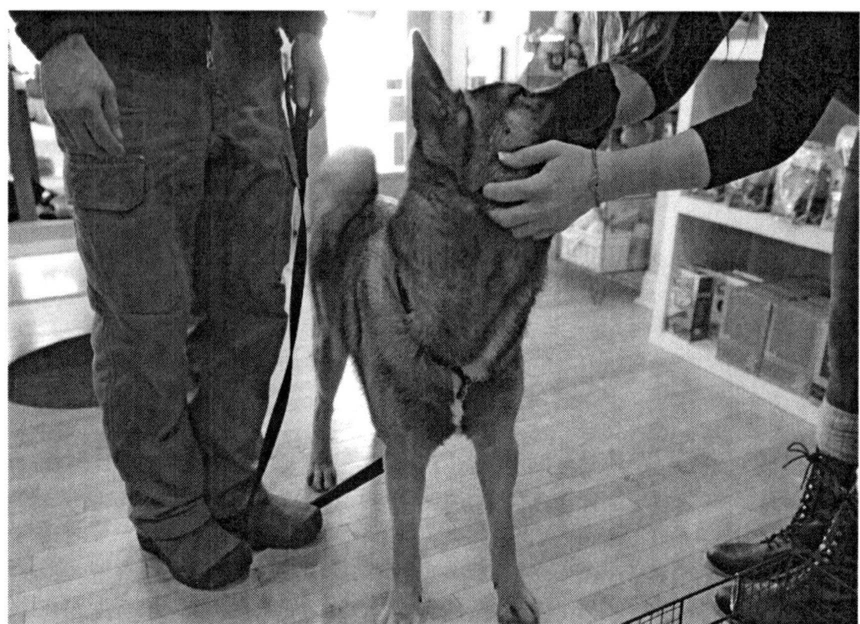

Stepping on your dog's leash at the midpoint is subtle (can you even tell that he's doing it?) and allows your dog to greet people while keeping all four paws on the ground.

let the midpoint of the leash dangle down close to the ground and plant your foot in the middle of it. This allows your dog enough room to stand comfortably but not enough room that he can launch himself at the person. Tell the person about your dog's "cool trick" (the arm-cross sit), and give your dog a treat when she executes it properly. The friendly stranger can then pet your dog while you keep your foot on the leash to prevent any further jumping.

In a perfect world, everyone who wanted to meet your dog would allow you to go through the finer points of attract/repel training. Unfortunately, that rarely happens, so the "leash-anchor" trick is an easy way to keep your dog from practicing an inappropriate behavior.

six

SHYNESS AND SOCIALIZATION

Most puppies seem ready to take on the world at all times, curious about every leaf that falls and every person that passes. In order to raise a well-rounded canine citizen, we need to take advantage of our puppies' natural curiosity and expose them to as many dog-friendly adventures as possible before they turn fourteen weeks old. Socialization is one of the most critical aspects of early development. Without a well-rounded socialization plan, puppies can grow into dogs that have crippling anxieties. I learned this lesson firsthand when I adopted Sumner at a year old. He spent his first year living in a crate with little exposure to other people, dogs, or new experiences, which translated into a dog that reacted with fear, aggression, or a combination of both when faced with anything that spooked him. (Thankfully, dog-friendly training made a huge difference in his life.)

Some puppies seem to come hardwired with shyness. They hang back when faced with new experiences and retreat when anyone reaches for them. Shyness is a mix of nature *and* nurture, so it's difficult to pinpoint the exact causes of it. A puppy that comes from a shy parent is more likely to exhibit similar behavioral traits, but it's also possible for a litter to have a mixture of withdrawn and outgoing puppies.

It's doubly important to socialize puppies that seem less outgoing, but the challenge is doing it in a way that the puppy feels comfortable and confident. The goal is to gently expose the shy puppy to potential stressors in such a way that the puppy learns to feel confident no matter her surroundings.

Case Study: Sara bought her Papillion puppy Belle from a breeder she found online. Because she lived more than ten hours away from the breeder, she wasn't able to meet the parents or see how the puppy was raised. She didn't have much communication with the breeder other than talking about her payment, but she did get a few cute photos of Belle posed on a furry pink blanket. The breeder shipped the ten-week-old puppy to Sara with assurances that she did it all the time and had never had a problem with pups flying in the cargo hold of an airplane. When Sara picked

Shy puppies need a slow and gentle socialization plan so that they can learn to feel more confident in new situations.

Belle up at the airport she discovered that the puppy had soiled her crate during the flight, but despite being coated in waste Belle wasn't willing to come out to meet Sara.

A few days later Belle received a clean bill of health at the vet. The puppy trembled during the entire exam. Sara took the vet's advice to keep Belle away from other dogs and public areas where dogs might visit until she completed her full series of vaccinations. Once Belle received the last shot Sara occasionally took her out, either carrying her in her arms or in a cushy dog bag. Any time they encountered another dog, Sara placed a protective arm around Belle and turned her body slightly away. "She's shy," Sara said as a way of explaining the seemingly antisocial behavior. Belle rarely tried to interact with other dogs or people. Instead, she retreated down in her carry bag, or buried her head in the crook of Sara's arm. Sometimes she even whimpered when a dog came too close to her. When a friendly Doberman tried to sneak a sniff of Belle from behind, Sara jumped and shouted at the dog's owner. "Your dog is scaring my dog! Please get it away!"

Any time someone wanted to meet Belle, Sara demurred, "She's really shy, she doesn't like people touching her." Belle whimpered, trembled, and hid whenever something frightened her. Unfortunately, it didn't take much. Belle lived in a state of suspended animation, carried in her person's arms high above any of the stress of everyday life.

What Does Fear Look Like?

Sara knew that Belle was fearful as demonstrated by the dog's hiding, jumping up to be held, and nervousness around other dogs. It's likely that Belle exhibited other more subtle signs of fearfulness that Sara missed. Picking up on these less obvious indicators of stress can help to avoid further reactivity. Understanding when your dog is feeling uncomfortable can enable you to take the appropriate steps to diffuse a potentially stressful situation. Fear can be expressed in many ways, including: **Tucked tail:** Tail carriage gives a great deal of information about a dog's emotional state. A fearful dog will keep her tail plastered between her legs. **Yawning:** Yawning is a contextual behavior. A tired dog will yawn at the end of a long day. A stressed dog will yawn when faced with something that makes it uncomfortable, like another dog that comes too close. **Lip licking:** Little tongue flicks around the mouth, or "lizard tongue," can indicate when a dog is feeling nervous. **Stress panting:** Another contextual behavior. A dog that has been running around and needs to cool off will naturally pant. A dog that breaks into a wide pant without a temperature or activity-level change is probably reacting to a stressful stimulus. **Whale eye:** A fearful dog will turn her head away from what is scaring her but will keep her eyes fixed on the stimulus. The whites of the eye become visible in the corners. **Stillness:** Refraining from moving at all can indicate that a dog is shutting down because of fear.

Possible Outcome One: At a year old, Belle acts helpless any time she encounters new scenarios. Belle hides in her carry bag when Sara brings friends over, and no amount of coaxing can get her to come out. When Sara reaches in and pulls Belle out of the bag, the dog immediately runs out of the room and hides. During walks outside, Belle stays close enough to Sara that she nearly trips over the dog. If a motorcycle or truck passes, the dog jumps up on Sara, asking to be carried. Sara always complies. When they encounter other dogs, Belle runs away with her tail tucked between her legs, even if the dog just glances at her from a distance. Sara went to a dog-training class when Belle hit eight months and had to drop out because all Belle did was hide under a chair. Frustrated, Sara gives up trying to "fix" Belle and finds ways to work around her nervous dog.

Possible Outcome Two: At about four months, Belle starts barking when she sees other dogs. When a dog walks over to meet her she stands very still for a moment and then lunges at the dog, seemingly without warning. Embarrassed, Sara scolds Belle halfheartedly. Walking Belle is difficult because she's reactive any time she sees a dog. When Belle barks, Sara simply picks her up and turns in the other direction, all the while trying to soothe her anxious dog. Because Belle is such a gorgeous dog, people always want to pet her. Belle has other ideas, though, and lets out a low growl any time someone reaches toward her, particularly men. Sara brings Belle to a small dog boutique to fit her for a new harness, and when the clerk attempts to slide it over her head, Belle lets out a cacophony of barks and growls that make the woman jump back in fear.

Belle's early fearfulness morphed into a lifelong handicap. Though it's difficult to pinpoint the reason that she turned out to be such a nervous dog (Did she have fearful parents? Was it her early upbringing? A combination of both?), it's likely that Sara could have avoided, or at the very least tempered, some of Belle's initial fears. What warning signs did Sara miss, and how could she have avoided Belle's extreme fearfulness?

Socialization Basics for Shy Puppies

Puppies go through a critical socialization period between eight and fourteen weeks of age (some say the period starts to wind down at twelve weeks) where they learn to relate to stimuli in the world. Puppies within this age range are more open to new experiences, as this is a time when sociability normally outweighs fear. Encouraging your puppy to have positive interactions with a variety of different types of people, animals, sounds, locations, and events before she turns fourteen weeks old can help her grow into a dog with excellent coping mechanisms. The well-socialized dog meets the world with an open, adaptable temperament.

A dog's social IQ isn't just related to her early life, though. Genetics also play a role in a dog's temperament. Sara wasn't able to meet Belle's parents, so she had no idea if the parents were socially confident dogs or not. In addition, she wasn't able to see the type of environment in which her puppy was raised. Belle might have faced a double whammy of nervous parents coupled with a breeder who didn't take the time to do any early socialization and handling with the pups. Like many dogs, particularly rescue dogs, Belle's early life was a black box. That said, Sara could have taken steps to socialize her dog to counteract any of the early shyness she noticed in Belle. Though it's impossible to say whether Belle's shyness could be completely eradicated through socialization, engaging in low-stress socialization in a variety of settings might have substantially lessened it.

Although some veterinarians still advise keeping puppies home until they've completed their full series of vaccinations, doing so places the puppy at the far end of the socialization window. Sara believed that it was in her puppy's best interest to keep her at home until the vaccination series was complete, but the social isolation only increased Belle's fearfulness. The fact is, the risk of undersocialization far outweighs the risk of infectious disease. Many veterinarians have revised their policies on socialization to recommend beginning the process once a puppy has received her first round of vaccinations and a deworming. Early socialization is critical because it reduces a dog's risk of "growing into" behavior problems later in life like fear and aggression, which are two of the most common reasons dogs are relinquished to shelters.

When we brought Olive home at eight weeks, I knew I had no choice but to throw her in the deep end of the socialization pool. I didn't want to leave her at home while Millie and I went to the store (particularly because of her housetraining challenges), so she started coming to work with us immediately. This was a potentially risky socialization plan because of the number of dogs that visit the store every day. To comfort myself, I made a sweeping generalization about the type of people that live in my town and visit my shop. I assumed that because it's a cosmopolitan area, it was likely that most of the dogs surrounding us would have been fully vaccinated. It's not a gamble that I would necessarily suggest to my clients, but for us it paid off. Now a year old, Olive welcomes every human and dog to the store with a positive attitude. (Granted, sometimes when she sees the first dog of

Have Dog Will Travel

You might be surprised to discover how many businesses welcome dogs. Obviously pet supply stores top the list, but have you thought about taking your puppy to:

- the bank
- the dry cleaner
- garden centers
- outdoor cafes
- toy stores
- the florist
- office supply stores
- outdoor shopping plazas
- home improvement stores

Some of the options listed above might be "information overload" for a shy puppy. Take into consideration that the noise at a dry cleaner or the crowds in a home improvement store might be too much for a nervous pup to handle right off the bat.

the day, her version of "positive attitude" means excited barking.) She's unflappable no matter what type of human bends down to meet her. People in hats, people with walkers, people loaded down with shopping bags, big burly men, toddlers . . . she receives everyone with the same broad wag of greeting. (And unfortunately, the occasional jump.) She greets dogs with similar aplomb, even the ones that play too roughly for her taste like the boxer mix described on page 54.

Although shy puppies aren't the norm, I've worked with enough of them over the years to recognize that they're out there in force. I can recall one shy Jack Russell Terrier mix that was so nervous about interacting with me that it took two weeks before she allowed me to be in the same room while we trained! (I spent the first two sessions coaching her person from the hallway.) The intensity of a puppy's fearfulness can vary greatly. Some pups conquer their fears quickly; they're young enough that the anxieties aren't entrenched yet. Others seem preprogrammed to react with intense fearfulness, like a puppy that attended one of my socialization classes a few years ago. No matter how calmly she was approached by another dog, even if they were the only two dogs in the room, she was unwilling to interact.

Socialization Baby Steps

Socializing a puppy that seems shy from the get-go requires a different set of rules. The goal is to gently introduce your puppy to as many different types of sights, sounds, people, and places before the window of socialization begins to close (and continue beyond that time, of course), but to do so in a way that doesn't cause her to "shut down" from fear. The good news is that this process can be fun, even with a less-than-outgoing pup! Map out places near your home that are dog friendly and can offer positive experiences for your puppy. The definition of "positive experience" can vary depending on the puppy in question. Avoid taking your shy puppy to places that might cause her to feel overwhelmed, like a bus stop surrounded by eager children, or at a ball game. That's not to say that the shy puppy should completely avoid potentially stressful situations. The idea is to begin the socialization process by visiting predictable settings in which your shy puppy can learn to feel confident, and then working up to environments that might be more stressful. That might mean going to the coffee shop with outdoor seating during an off-peak time, like 3:00 P.M. on a Wednesday instead of 8:00 A.M. on a Monday morning.

Once there, you and your new puppy shouldn't have a problem attracting attention, but the challenge is making sure that people interact with her properly. Always keep in mind that you are your dog's advocate. If someone approaches your puppy in an inappropriate fashion (for example,

This shy puppy's body language suggests that she's overwhelmed by the attention from the children.

if they scream excitedly when they see her or try to pick her up without asking), use your body to block the person by stepping in front of your puppy, and then explain that you're doing special "shy puppy" training. This is where it gets difficult. Wanting to enlist the help of a friendly stranger and then placing demands on the person doesn't always go over well, so be prepared to sweet talk the person through proper greeting etiquette. Instruct him that the best way to interact with your puppy is to kneel down facing slightly away from her, and then toss a treat toward your pup. Tell him to refrain from reaching out to your puppy. If your puppy seems confident with the person and approaches willingly, then he may pet her. If your puppy retreats after the person touches, thank him for helping out, and move on with her.

Consider potential stressors when visiting new locations. It's a wonderful idea to take your shy puppy to your bank during off-peak hours, but is it possible that the slick floors will frighten her? Will she be comfortable going through a revolving door? (It's impossible to predict every scary interaction when out in the real world, but giving it some thought will help prevent obvious run-ins.) Once again, the idea is not to shelter your puppy completely from interactions with potential stressors, but to break down the "monster" into tiny digestible pieces. Don't expect your puppy to cross the slick floor the very first time she encounters it. (For this reason, don't take your shy puppy on errands and expect to complete them all.

Taking the Stairs

Many puppies, shy or not, are nervous about attempting stairs. Teaching a puppy to feel confident about stairs is a simple process. Place your puppy on the lowest step, and then put a treat on the ground below the puppy. Praise your puppy when she moves from the bottom step to the ground to get the treat. Repeat the process a few times, facing your dog in different direction on the step with each attempt. Then try the next step up, placing treats on the bottom step as well as the floor. Praise your dog for her bravery, and then wrap up the training session. The next time you attempt stairs with your puppy, start on the bottom step once again, and quickly move to the next step up.

Socialization trips should be for socialization, so then there's no problem if you have to abort your mission.) Instead, stay on a rug near the door and place a tempting treat right on the edge rug near the slick floor. Praise your puppy for grabbing it, and then plant another one a few inches off the rug and on the floor. Praise your dog again, and give her a quick break by giving her a treat while she has four paws on the rug. Finish the session by placing a treat far enough off the rug so that your puppy has to place one

Stairs can be daunting for pups, but starting at the bottom can make it much less scary.

paw on the slick floor in order to reach the treat. Give your puppy a ton of praise when she completes this step, and wrap up training. You might find that the next time you visit the bank, your puppy is more willing to attempt walking on the slick floor.

Identify and De-Stress Triggers

If you notice your puppy acting hesitant with a certain type of person—a man in a hat or a toddler, for example—file the information away in your mental "to do" folder. Continue to let your puppy interact with people around whom she feels comfortable, but do your best to prevent the "scary" people from forcing themselves on your puppy. How do you do that? It can be awkward, but tell the person something like, "We're working on getting her used to guys in hats—she's a little afraid. Thanks for understanding!" Again, it's not that you want to sequester your puppy from things that scare her; it's that you want to be able to control the intensity of the greeting in order to transform something uncomfortable into something positive for your puppy.

After you've identified a list of scary folks, you should begin the counterconditioning and desensitization process. Counterconditioning and desensitization can change your puppy's perception of something or someone that she sees as unpleasant into something that she views as positive. First, try to determine your puppy's "threshold" for comfort, meaning, how far away the scary person must stand so that your puppy notices him but doesn't react fearfully. This can be difficult to gauge, but make the assumption that the distance is farther than you think. Once you've identified the appropriate distance (A block? Ten feet?), ask your trigger person to step into view from that far away, and the moment your puppy notices him give your puppy bits of a delicious "special-occasion" treat. Don't be stingy! You should feed your pup little bits of treats over and over while the person is in sight. Then wait a few seconds (don't expose your puppy to the stimulus for too long) and have the person step out of sight again. The moment that the trigger disappears, stop feeding treats.

The idea is that the scary person standing at a nonthreatening distance is paired with a very high value reward. Person appears, pup gets delicious goodies, person goes away, treats stop. Repeat the process at the safe distance several times, until your puppy sees the person appear and looks to you as if to say, "Where are my goodies?" This is a very meaningful moment in the training process! It indicates that change is happening: your puppy has begun to pair something aversive—the scary man—with something positive—treats. Keep in mind that once you begin this training process, you *never* want your dog to have a nervous reaction to the stimulus. If your puppy refuses treats that she was eating earlier in the

Maintain a buffer of distance between your puppy and the person she's afraid of to help her remain calm and confident.

session, it means that you've pushed too hard and your puppy has shut down. Your puppy should remain at a calm threshold, and should only get excited about the possibility of more treats!

The next step is to gradually bring the scary person closer in increments. Ask your bearded or hat-wearing helper to step out of sight, pause, and then reappear a few steps closer to where you and your puppy are standing. Feed your puppy treats continuously while the person is visible, again making the connection between the stimulus and the food. Continue asking the person to step out of sight and reappear at the safe distance in short intervals. When you see that same "where-are-my-goodies?" reaction from your puppy, ask the person to step out of sight and then reappear at an even closer distance. Continue decreasing the distance of the stimulus from your puppy, making sure to get the "goodies" look at each location before you have the person move closer.

It's helpful to take minibreaks during the session rather than repeatedly pushing the scary person on her. Work until you see a "where-are-my-treats?" look, then stroll for a bit. Ask your puppy to do a sit for you, play a little game, and then get back to work. This is like hitting the "reset" button.

In the real world, scary strangers don't stand still at a distance and wait for instructions, so you want to round out the training process with your puppy by changing the intensity of the stimulus. If you worked on getting your puppy to accept a solo man in a hat, try gradually exposing her to two men in hats at the safe distance away. Work through the process in the same fashion, with the two men moving closer after you've gotten the "goodies" look from your puppy. Your puppy's perception of the stimulus will change not only based on her distance from it, but also on whether the stimulus is making noise, or moving, or wearing something strange like a big puffy coat, or is in a group as opposed to solo. If possible, work through every iteration of the stimulus possible, trying to envision how it appears in the real world. If your puppy is afraid of children, work through the process until the children can move around and act as children normally do.

Make sure to change your location frequently as you work through the counterconditioning process. You want her to learn that the guy with the

Extreme "Meet the Puppy"

There's a strange phenomenon with some toy puppy owners; I call it "here's my puppy" syndrome. Toy puppy owners stop by my store carrying their new baby in their arms (usually a Yorkie or a Chihuahua), and when I comment about how adorable the trembling puppy is, the owner says, "here," and hands the nervous dog over to me without preamble. The trainer in me is usually shrieking in my head, "Oh no, your puppy doesn't want me to hold her! This is really freaking her out! Take her back, take her back!" I cover my surprise with a few quick words of praise and hand the puppy back to her person. It's an unfortunate lesson for the puppy that I want no part of.

I'm not a fan of carrying toy dogs everywhere, particularly when it comes time to meet new people. It's more natural to allow the dog to approach a stranger at her own pace rather than thrusting her at the person. Plus, if the puppy expresses any reactivity to the stranger like growling while in her person's arms and the stranger backs away, that growly reaction is reinforced. The puppy will quickly learn, "If I don't want anyone to touch me while my person is holding me, all I have to do is growl and the stranger will back off!"

beard makes treats happen at the park, the shopping plaza, and the coffee shop!

This same counterconditioning process can be used with inanimate objects as well, like brooms and suitcases. If your puppy is frightened of brooms, ask your nonthreatening helper (preferably not a bearded man wearing a hat!) to stand at the safe distance holding the broom completely still. Feed your puppy treats, and after a few seconds ask the helper to take the broom out of sight. Next, ask the person to reappear with the broom at the safe distance until your puppy offers you the excited "there's-the-broom-where-are-my-goodies?" look. Continue through the process, moving the broom and helper closer each time, always looking for your puppy's "goodies" response before you move on. Once your puppy welcomes the broom at close range, start the process over at the safe distance, but this time ask your helper to sweep the broom once. (Don't jump from a still broom to an actual sweep-up session, though.) Run through the process once again, until your puppy is comfortable with a single sweep close by. Then start the process over at the safe distance and ask your helper to mimic what real sweeping up looks like.

As is true of any training, don't overdo it after your initial success. It's easy to get excited when you see your pup's reaction to the stimulus change, but the worst thing you could do is push your pup to the breaking point by continuing the process before she's ready. If you're doing it correctly, this type of training is not exciting, and it looks nothing like the kind of dramatic personality changes that happen on TV dog-training shows. It's methodical and predictable for both you and your puppy. Unfortunately, there is no rule of thumb as to how quickly you should be able to progress through the process. Let your puppy's reactions be your guide. If during training your puppy displays any of the postures mentioned on page 83, wrap up the lesson for the day.

Find Appropriate Canine Friends

While socialization classes are a great idea for most puppies, shy pups present a unique challenge. Your puppy needs to learn about etiquette from other dogs, but often the rough-and-tumble play at a typical socialization class can prove to be too much for a nervous puppy. While the worried puppy might learn *some* lessons by hanging back and watching the fun, it's still vitally important for the puppy to have "paws-on" interactions with other dogs to avoid the types of reactions that Belle exhibited in both of the potential outcomes.

Two of my recent private clients took their shy puppy, Benny, to a few socialization classes, only to have the puppy run away in fear any time a

This position, a play bow, is an invitation to dogs and people alike to have some fun!

dog tried to approach him. They quit the class but knew that they had to take steps to get Benny comfortable around other dogs. My dogs, Millie and Olive, both have exceptional shy-dog skills when they're "off duty" at the store, so I invited Benny and his people to stop by early on a Saturday morning to try to gauge exactly what they were dealing with. We met outside the store on neutral ground at a grassy patch, keeping the leashes as loose as possible while the dogs inspected each other. (Tight leashes can increase stress.) After a few long-distance sniffs, we went back to the store for some off-leash fun.

Millie and Olive took turns calmly approaching Benny. When Olive got a bit too pushy for Benny's liking, I said, "Nice and easy, please," and she backed off immediately. (I was impressed by how well she listened that morning! Millie, on the other hand, is almost always perfect.) Benny allowed them to inspect him, and sniffed their rear ends when they turned their backs to him. He was indeed shy, but not crippled by it. After the first round of sniffing I wanted to get my dogs focused on something other than Benny, so I grabbed their favorite noisy toy. They immediately started playing near Benny while he looked on with interest. He never backed away from them, even when they became vocal. A few times he even walked toward them and offered a play bow, the universal invitation to play, where the dog puts the front part of his body (his chest and elbows) on the ground and keeps the rear end up in the air. (He wasn't quite sure

Finding the Right Fit

Just because one puppy play group didn't work out for your puppy doesn't mean that *none* of them will. Unfortunately, some socialization classes are more free-for-all than constructive dog-dog interactions. If your puppy wasn't willing to get out and play in a class because there were too many dogs or too much drama, find out if there are other puppy programs in your area. Often another mix of dogs can make a difference. A well-run puppy socialization class takes the sizes and ages of the participants into account, grouping pups according to size and play style. The puppies are monitored carefully by an instructor well-versed in canine body language, and inappropriate play is stopped.

what to do when they tried to take him up on his offer to play, though!) It was clear that Benny was interested in Millie and Olive, and willing to interact little by little.

We took a walk around the block together and Benny strained to keep up with Millie and Olive the whole time. They engaged in some communal sniffing, and to any observer they probably looked like three friends out for a stroll. When we returned to the store, though, it became clear that the weight of what we were doing was making Benny tired. He opted to sit in his person's lap and watch Millie and Olive play. Rather than push him beyond his comfort zone, we decided to wrap up the session. Benny's people were heartened by their dog's reactions to Millie and Olive—they had never seen him get that close to other dogs before!

Socializing a shy puppy requires finding puppies or adult dogs that have exceptional dog skills. Unfortunately, most puppies are still learning dog skills, hence the need for socialization! That said, dog-savvy puppies do exist. As a puppy, Millie could alter her play style to match that of any dog that walked in the door. She was game to chase, wrestle, or play tug with a toy—whatever the other dog wanted. I watched her teach many a shy puppy how to play, coaxing each one gently with a toy, or rolling on her back to expose her belly as if to say, "I'm harmless, now come and get me!" I can recall how Millie gentled one very shy Aussie puppy into a short wrestling match, altering her typical moves to keep the dog from getting nervous. The next time the puppy came to visit they wrestled with slightly more vigor, and then all subsequent visits found the two of them grappling like professionals. As a puppy, Olive had less finesse than Millie, but she has grown into an admirable play buddy, ready to back off if requested by the dog or by me.

As you socialize your shy puppy with other dogs, take care to find friends that don't overwhelm him.

Introducing your shy puppy to other pups with this type of open welcoming temperament can help to pave the way to friendship. A puppy that might be a good match for a shy puppy is one that is similar in size, and has had experience playing with other dogs of all temperaments and types. Though larger-breed puppies can sometimes be a good fit, their size and lack of coordination might frighten an anxious puppy. Signs that your puppy is enjoying the play with a gentle ambassador puppy include readily coming back to the game after taking a break, following the ambassador puppy when she walks away, and asking for play when the ambassador puppy pauses. The ambassador puppy should be able to recognize when the shy puppy wants to cool down or, at the very least, listen to her person when called away from the other pup. Obviously, signs like running away from the ambassador puppy or hiding are indicators that your puppy needs a rest. Initial play sessions should be short and should end before either party becomes overtired. Play sessions with an appropriate adult dog can also help to draw out a shy puppy. Much like the ambassador puppy, the adult dog friend should be well-versed in dog-play etiquette and able to cope if the shy puppy suddenly comes out of her shell and acts like a typical puppy. (Many adult dogs don't tolerate youthful shenanigans. A harsh correction from the adult friend might set a shy puppy back.)

The more positive dog-dog interactions your shy puppy has, the better off she'll be. Dogs don't generalize well, so one successful play date won't turn your apprehensive puppy into a social butterfly. Don't give up completely on puppy play groups, either. You might find that after several successful play sessions with appropriate dogs, your puppy can tolerate the excitement of a well-run group play class.

Meet the Puppy Party

There's a great big world to explore outside your front door, but it's also important to welcome strangers into your puppy's "safe zone," your home. One way to do this is to host a puppy-socialization party. Usually, puppy-socialization parties are boisterous affairs, where the new puppy is adored by groups of people in your home. Shy pups require a more intimate party, with just one or two guests initially. The good news is that it's usually easier to instruct friends and relatives about the finer points of shy-puppy handling than it is strangers!

Start off by inviting a few friends over, and let them know that they should ignore your puppy when they first enter. Bring everyone into a comfortable room, and sit on the floor. Give your guests treats for your puppy. Allow your puppy to investigate your friends, but ask them to refrain from reaching out to her for a short time. Ask them to place treats on the ground around where they're sitting. If the puppy takes the treats but stretches out her body keeping her back feet as far away as possible, she's demonstrating that she's not feeling 100 percent comfortable about the interaction. If your puppy takes the treats and her entire body remains close to your friend, have the person hold out a treat in the palm of their hand and offer it to your puppy. Ask your friend to refrain from petting your puppy until the dog is choosing to remain close to where the person is sitting on the ground.

Work up to walking around your home with your guests, standing in the kitchen, and doing everything that guests would normally do when visiting. Have your friends toss treats on the ground for your puppy if she follows along with you. If she opts to hang back, don't force the issue and *make* her hang out close to your guests. As with all shy-puppy training, allow your dog to set the pace.

If possible, welcome the same guests to your house again before inviting anyone new over. You should be able to progress through the initial steps quickly, and hopefully your puppy will recognize your friends as friends of hers as well!

If you invite people over and your shy pup disappears under a couch or behind a corner, allow her that social distance. It might help to "Hansel and Gretel" a few high-value treats on the floor from her hiding spot to where you and your guests are hanging out to encourage her to explore, but don't require that she come out. You can facilitate some interaction or, at the very least, observation of the "scary" people by tethering a treat-stuffed activity toy a short distance away from where you and your guests are sitting. That way your dog is physically present in the room with you (though she can escape if she wants to), occupied by something wonderful that, with repetition, she might learn to associate with visitors.

Support or Ignore Fear Reactions?

Once upon a time people who owned nervous pups were told to ignore their dogs' fearful reactions, because if they acknowledged them with soothing words, the fearful behavior would accidentally be reinforced. My take on the issue is to help the puppy understand, through words and tone of voice, that whatever is scaring them is really no big deal. It's a way of letting the puppy know that everything is okay, but it takes the overly comforting tones out and instead relies on a "*nothing* to worry about!" approach.

Olive was beautifully socialized during her early months with us, but despite my best efforts, she is sound sensitive. If something drops and makes a loud noise, like a frying pan, she disappears. When she peeks her head around the corner to see if the rest of us are still alive, I'll say, "Olive, no worries! Everything is *fine!* It's just a silly old pot!" My tone of voice is upbeat and playful. I continue praising her as she takes a few tentative steps toward the scary pot. I allow her to approach at her own speed, and when she finally bridges the gap and comes close enough to sniff the item, I say, "See, no big deal! It's nothing." She then usually checks out the pot to see if there's anything in it to eat.

While it's tempting to coo over a nervous puppy as one would to a baby, I find it more helpful to take an upbeat, positive approach. Even though puppies might not understand the exact *meaning* of our words, the tone makes the intent behind them clear. No matter the scenario, whether the puppy is encountering a scary man with a beard from a distance as described on pages 89–91, or attempting to navigate a patch of unfamiliar terrain like sand, encourage your puppy in such a way that you are instilling confidence with your words and not pacifying.

When Is Socialization Over?

You've done an excellent job helping your shy puppy to feel more confident in a variety of places with a variety of people. Your shy puppy is now acting much more normal. Congratulations! Though you've done a great deal of work to help your shy puppy feel more confident, you're never truly done socializing your dog, shy or not. Socialization is like a muscle: if you use it and work it, the muscle will stay strong and serve you well. If you let it languish, the muscle will atrophy. Even though a puppy's window of socialization eventually closes, that doesn't mean that the need for socialization ends, particularly for a puppy that started off with a shy disposition.

When your shy puppy is acting more confident in formerly stressful situations, take advantage of her newfound bravery and get out there! Walk her in new neighborhoods, take her to play with dog friends next door, run errands with her, and enjoy the new freedom that your hard work has provided. Remember to keep a pocket full of savory treats, just in case you encounter something unusual or need to reward for a job well done, and continue to monitor your dog for signs of stress. You've done the work to bolster your dog's confidence; now keep up with it to ensure that she never backslides.

part two

LIFE WITH FIDO

Unfortunately, behavior problems don't stop at puppyhood. Challenges often develop as our dogs mature—they "grow into" their problems—and the issues that seemed easy to deal with in puppyhood become overwhelming. The concept of mindful interactions is just as applicable in adulthood. The simple questions "Do I like this behavior? Do I want it to continue?" remain relevant with a mature dog.

It's rare that a dog "unlearns" a negative behavior. Clients with older dogs ask me, "Will my dog stop pulling when he mellows out at three years old?" or "Will she ever stop running away from me?" Unfortunately, these types of problems rarely, if ever, disappear without some sort of intervention. So let's get to it!

seven

TRAINING PROBLEM ONE: LEASH PULLING

Leash pulling is a "creeper" challenge—it sneaks up on you! It typically starts in puppyhood, because allowing a ten-pound puppy to drag you down the street doesn't seem like a big deal. The behavior is cemented early on because the puppy learns, "I pull, and they follow. This is great!" The problem becomes apparent as the small dog enters adolescence and the baby puppy begins to gain some strength. Suddenly, that cute little puppy is a sled dog on a mission. You do your best to hold on for the ride, but it's not easy, as your dog's strong neck and lower center of gravity makes for an efficient tow truck. Over time, leash pulling can become painful for both the dog and the person at the other end of the leash.

Case Study: Ted adopted Gunner the Brittney Spaniel mix when he was just under a year old. Gunner was relinquished to a rescue organization because of his former owner's allergies, so Ted was able to learn a great deal about his new dog from the notes that came with him. The dog was well loved and had a sweet but typically energetic disposition. Ted took Gunner to a training class and was pleased to discover how quickly his dog picked up on all of the basic cues like "sit," "down," and "come." Gunner even excelled at "heel" while in the training room, though his walks to and from the facility were another story. Gunner pulled, hard.

Gunner graduated from the class with honors since his leash-pulling habit was their dirty little secret. Ted could never get Gunner to heel while they took walks around town, even though he continued jerking the metal collar and saying "Heel! Heel!" Sometimes Gunner winced when Ted delivered a correction, but most of the time he just powered through the tugs at his neck and kept pulling. Even though Gunner only weighed forty pounds, Ted could barely hold on when he pulled at full tilt. (Which was pretty much all of the time.)

Possible Outcome One: Ted had always had a bad back, and he soon realized that his twice-daily walks with Gunner were making it worse. Not only did Gunner pull, but he also ran after any other living thing they encountered during walks, like squirrels or other dogs. Ted tried every possible contraption to decrease Gunner's pulling, from head collars to antipull harnesses, but they usually only stopped it for a few walks before Gunner was back to dragging Ted down the street. Because of Ted's pain (and the fact that he didn't enjoy getting pulled around for forty-five minutes), their walks became shorter and shorter, until Gunner got only a quick walk around the block to do his business. Bored by the lack of exercise, Gunner took to ripping up shoes and acting out of control around the house.

Possible Outcome Two: Frustrated by Gunner's pulling—which he viewed as insubordination—Ted goes back to his remedial training lessons and gives Gunner frequent corrections during their walks. When the dog reaches the end of the leash, Ted yanks Gunner back with such force that the dog's front feet lift off the ground. One day Gunner spots a squirrel on the sidewalk ahead of them while Ted is distracted. He takes off running at top speed, only to have Ted anticipate the dash and pull back on the leash with both hands just as Gunner hits the end of the leash. The yank flips Gunner with such force that he lands on his back on the sidewalk. He remains on the ground for a few moments, dazed, and then gets up slowly. Gunner coughs persistently after the fall, and when Ted notices that one of Gunner's pupils looks different than the other, he decides to take him to the vet. He discovers that Gunner has soft tissue damage, probably due to the painful dash after the squirrel.

How could Ted have addressed Gunner's entrenched pulling habit? Was the choke chain doing the trick for the pair, or should they have explored other training options?

Consider Your Equipment

Although choke chains were the only training option for years, they're now considered outdated equipment by trainers who have embraced a more dog-friendly approach to dog training. Training with a choke collar relies on training with pain. Even though trainers who use choke chains say that dogs respond to the sound of the metal links clinking together (the leash "check"), the fact is that the collar delivers a painful pinch around the neck each time it's tightened. Instead of rewarding the dog for what he's doing *right* during a leash walk, as is the case with dog-friendly dog training, correction-based training requires the trainer to punish the dog every time he does something *wrong*. Often, the amount of force necessary to make a behavior-changing correction is more than the average dog owner can stomach, so the dog ends up dealing with persistent painful jerks during walks that have little effect on the dog's behavior. Choke chains can do more harm than good, so if you're currently walking your sled dog on one, ask yourself, "Is this tool working for us?"

Your leash also plays a role in your dog's pulling habit. Although flexible leashes seem wonderful—they give your dog fifteen feet of freedom to explore and burn off excess energy!—a flexible leash can actually *encourage* a dog to pull. Flexible leashes have a tension mechanism in them to keep the extra length from dragging on the ground, so unless the leash is locked, there is always pressure between the dog and the handle. Dogs have "opposition reflex," which means that when something pushes or pulls against them, their reflex is to push or pull in the opposite direction. Imagine a tight leash pulling back against your dog's collar. Based on opposition reflex, his natural inclination is to pull forward, thereby reinforcing the pulling!

I find that a fixed length leash between four to six feet long is a good fit for most dogs. Anything under four feet doesn't give your dog much room to find the perfect potty spot, and anything over six feet gives your dog more freedom than she needs on the typical walk. (Plus, it can be hard to juggle a leash that long.) Whether you select a nylon leash or leather is up to you; just be aware that leather can be a temptation for dogs that like to chew!

It should come as no surprise that treats are a major part of the training "equipment" necessary for leash training. Because you'll be competing with a variety of distractions during your walk, like squirrels, people, other dogs, blowing leaves, litter, cars, bikes, and scent molecules, you'll need a moist, stinky treat that your dog absolutely loves. (Cut your goodies up into tiny bits, as you're going to be giving a lot of them!) Make sure that the treats are accessible as you walk, since there's nothing worse than wanting to reward your dog for a job well done only to have to fumble to find the treat.

Finally, make sure to bring your positive attitude. Your dog isn't pulling on the leash to be insubordinate or dominant. She's pulling because it works for her, plain and simple. Although the techniques to curb leash pulling are straightforward, the process can be frustrating. It's easy to figure out what to do but hard to keep it up! Remaining mindful during your walks, and always noticing improvements in your dog's performance (even tiny improvements), will enable you to work through the everyday challenges of leash training more easily.

Additional Tools: Head Collars and Harnesses

A dog with an entrenched pulling habit can often benefit from "intervention" in the form of a no-pull harness or head collar. In addition, a dog guardian with mobility or strength issues (in a scenario where the dog outweighs the guardian, for example) can also benefit from the speedy behavioral change these training tools can provide. That said, harnesses and head collars don't teach the correct behavior, they merely prevent the dog from successfully engaging in pulling. When the tool comes off, the pulling remains.

A no-pull harness is different from a typical H-style harness in that it is designed to make pulling difficult if not impossible for the dog, whereas traditional harnesses, much like collars, merely provide a place to snap on the leash. No-pull harnesses are constructed so that the positioning of the leash clip—often in the middle of the chest—and the straps along the sides of the dog's body prevent pulling through leverage and pressure. A properly fitted no-pull harness can provide instant results in many dogs, though the dedicated puller might still be able to pull while wearing one. In my experience, no-pull harnesses usually work *immediately,* but if you don't see a quick reduction in pulling after putting one on your dog, it's not likely to help the dog in the long run. The dogs that benefit from wearing one usually have a short acclimation period when the dog will attempt to pull ahead and seem to say, "Huh! What's this?" Most dogs do not react dramatically to wearing a no-pull harness for the first time.

Head collars can also provide a quick fix, but they are more controversial than no-pull harnesses. A head collar looks like a muzzle because a strap is fitted around the dog's muzzle and behind the head. People unfamiliar with the tool might confuse it with a muzzle, which might cast the dog wearing

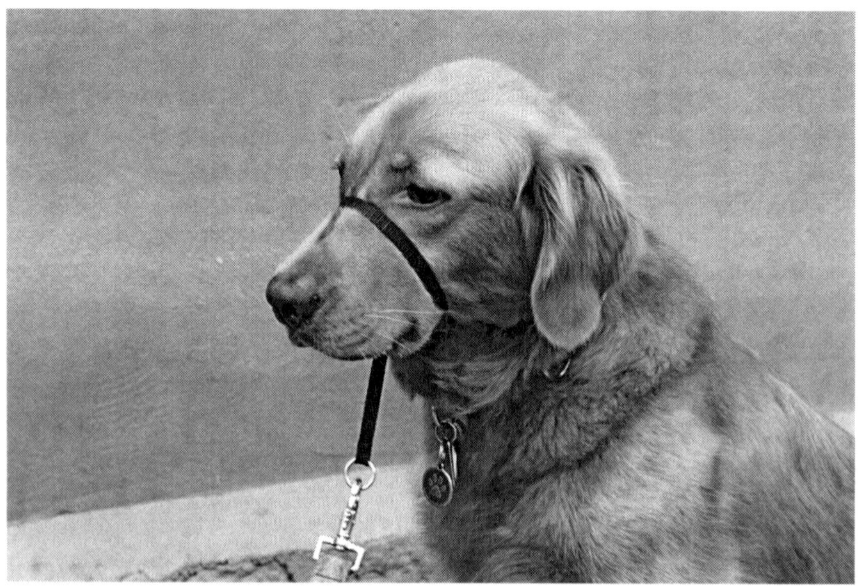

A no-pull head collar can quickly reduce pulling, but most dogs have a hard time getting used to wearing it.

it in an unflattering light. A properly fitted head collar is not a muzzle; a dog wearing one should be able to open its mouth completely in order to bite, drink, or pant.

A dog head collar functions in much the same way as a horse head collar does; if you can lead the animal's head, you can lead the body. Because the leash attaches beneath the dog's chin, it changes the fulcrum point of the leash. (It's important to use a leash with a light clasp when using a head collar, as a heavy clasp might weigh the dog's head down unnecessarily and cause her to try to fight it off.) *Most* dogs cannot pull their full body weight with their head, although some learn to stiffen their necks in order to do just that, thereby negating the tool's purpose.

In my experience, many dogs do not take to wearing a head collar without a struggle. The initial complete loss of freedom and unfamiliar sensation of the strap around the muzzle usually translates into a dog that bucks, rolls, and paws at the head collar in an attempt to get it off, off, *off!* This dramatic acclimation period can last for a few blocks during the dog's first walk wearing one, or it can take the dog days to adapt to the sensation. I've worked with a few dogs that exhibited such a dramatic reaction to the head collar that I opted not to use it. Wearing one shouldn't be tortuous for the dog! Even dogs that habituate to head collars can exhibit a pronounced "depression" while wearing it.

I consider no-pull harnesses and head collars tools that can help to quickly reduce if not eliminate pulling, but not solutions to the underlying problem. Granted, many people find a no-pull option that works for their dog and then give up trying to teach their dog to walk politely without it. That's certainly an option (and in certain households it might be a requirement), but I find that using a training tool in *addition* to doing leash training can help to curb even the most dedicated pullers.

Leash-Training Basics

I like to call leash training a marathon behavior; when you start working on it you're in it for the long run, particularly when you have an unrepentant puller. Unfortunately, there is no such thing as "training walks" and "everyday walks." You're on duty *every* time you take your dog outside for a walk, even if you didn't intend to train! I'll say it again: if you have the leash in one hand and your dog is attached to it, you're training.

One of the reasons I don't like sled-dog walks, or walks where the dog is at the end of the leash pulling as hard as possible, is that there's very little communication going on between dog and handler. It's almost as if the pulling dog doesn't notice that her person is on the other end of the leash—all she wants to do is continue covering ground. I think leash walks should be a "conversation" between dog and handler, where you meet the world as

Before You Begin

Polite leash manners should start the second you announce that it's time to go walk. Many dogs react to the sight of the leash with over-the-top enthusiasm (jumping, barking, running around) that makes it difficult to clip the leash to the collar, let alone commence with the walk. Allowing your dog to act insane before you begin a walk sets the tone for the rest of it, so teach your dog how to wait patiently as you get ready to go.

If your dog triggers when you say "walk" or anything similar, avoid saying it during the training phase. Simply go to your "leashing station," pick up the leash, and call your dog over. Ask her to sit. You probably won't get an immediate response because of her excitement for the pending walk (as well as her history of getting rewarded for acting like a goofball), so give her a short time to collect herself in order to do it. If she's not able to sit and she jumps or acts crazy, drop the leash and walk away. Wait a short time—as if you've decided not to take the walk after all—and then call your dog back to you and try again.

You might have to drop the leash several times before your dog understands that the only way she'll get to leave is if she sits calmly for leashing up. (Don't try this technique when it's a critical potty time!) When she finally does it, leash her up quickly and get out there. There's no need to give a treat for this behavior, as the opportunity to go out for a walk is enough. Ask everyone in the household to follow the same protocol, and in no time you'll have drama-free leash ups!

a team. In my world, polite leash walking is when your dog walks near you, but not necessarily in a perfect heel position. I find that forcing a dog to remain in heel—close to your leg and not veering away at all—is probably not much fun for the dog. Granted, heel can be helpful on a crowded city street, but asking for a heel on a casual walk doesn't allow your dog the joyful exploration and sniffing required for a "good" walk. When I work with my clients, our mutual goal is to train a dog that *chooses* to walk nearby (on one side of your body and not zigzagging in front of you), but also has the freedom to move off the path to sniff something if she wishes. It's a collaborative process that's fun for both parties. The leash is always loose, meaning that it has a curve in it at all times.

Using a "marker" like a clicker is a very effective way to tackle leash manners, as the sound is a clear way to help your dog understand when she's reacting appropriately. The clicker's distinct sound can cut through the environmental clutter outside, so you can promptly reward your dog no

When working on polite leash walking, use one hand for the clicker and the other hand for the treats. Deliver the treats from the hand closest to your dog.

matter how distracting it gets, whether you're trying to train around noisy garbage trucks or taunting squirrels. While the clicker is a powerful training tool during leash walks, juggling a leash, treats, and a clicker can be a challenge. It helps to designate one hand as the treat hand, and then use the other hand for the leash and clicker. Your treat hand should be positioned so that your dog doesn't have to step in front of you in order to collect the treat, as the two of you will end up tripping over each other. That means that if you're comfortable using your left hand for treats, your dog should walk on your left side as well. No matter which hand you designate as your treat hand, the other hand should hold both the leash and the clicker. That means that the leash will drape across your body as you walk, which might feel awkward at first but should become more comfortable as both you and your dog become familiar with the leash-walking basics. You should always keep one hand on the "trigger" (the clicker) when leash walking, so it's best to loop the leash around your hand a few times *underneath* the clicker.

If you opt to train without using a clicker, condition a word that takes the place of the sound of the clicker. I like to use the word "yup," as it's a short, precise sound. Teach the word indoors over the course of a few training sessions by asking your dog to sit and then saying "yup" right as her bottom

It helps to loop the leash around your hand and under the clicker, making it as tight as it feels comfortable for you.

hits the ground. Follow up with a treat. Repeat the process about a dozen times, until your dog understands that when you say "yup" it means that she's going to get paid with a food reward. I typically wean off the clicker to using a click word like "yup" when the dog understands the basic rules of the road, but if the clicker proves to be too challenging during walks, you can begin the process using a click word like "yup." The main drawback of using a click word? Your voice isn't as clear as the sound of the clicker, so you might have to work a little harder to get the word to register if your dog is distracted.

If possible, time your walks so that environmental distractions around are minimal. Walking during off-peak times helps to stack the deck in your favor, but I recognize that it's not always possible. That said, taking your walk just fifteen minutes earlier or later might make the difference between a traffic jam of dog friends on the sidewalk versus a quieter walk during which your dog is better able to focus on you. You can work up to more distracting walks once the two of you have the basics down.

Polite leash walking should begin immediately, before you even leave the house. If your dog runs out the door ahead of you and drags you, walk back to the door and begin again. You might have to repeat this step several times before your dog understands that rushing ahead isn't a viable strategy.

When the two of you are out the door, stand still for a moment. If your dog manages to stay close to you, let her know that she's got the right idea by clicking and treating her. If she is straining at the end of the leash and you're as good as a dead weight, stay still. Don't allow your dog to pull your arm out of its socket; keep your arm close to your body, and don't "give" by leaning toward where your dog is straining. Eventually, your dog will realize that she's not making progress and will glance at you. Capture this very important moment with a click and treat! Acknowledge your dog *any* time she withdraws her attention from the environmental distractions and focuses on you instead, as doing so underscores the idea that leash walking is a collaborative adventure.

Take a few steps. If your dog manages to walk without pulling, click and treat. In the beginning stages of the walk, *anything* other than pulling is worthy of reward, even if your dog is a few steps ahead of you or veering out to the side. Her behavior is click-worthy as long as the leash has a curve in it. (A straight leash is usually just a step away from being a tight leash.) It's tempting to want to reward only perfect examples of polite leash walking, but that's a potentially frustrating venture for both of you, as a dog with a history of leash pulling won't offer anything close to perfect walking at the outset. I often liken training to the "hot-and-cold" game we all played as children, in which one player tries to find a hidden object by getting clues from the other player. As the seeker gets closer to the hidden object, the other player says, "You're getting warmer, you're getting warmer." If the seeker is heading in the wrong direction the other player warns, "You're getting colder." In a way we're applying this same logic to leash training. The pulling dog is "cold" and therefore gets nothing from you (not even forward movement), but the dog that walks while keeping a gentle curve in the leash, even if she's not right by your side, is "getting warmer" and is told as much through clicks and treats. (You can further mirror the game by using extra-special treats like cheese when your dog is walking by your

Clicker Vocab

When I use the word *click*, I *always* mean *click and treat*. In my world, there is no such thing as the click without the treat. You certainly can give a treat without a click, but you should never give a click without a treat. Why? The click is the behavioral marker and the predictor of the treat, which is payment for a job well done. If you click but don't follow up with a treat, the power of the click will be diluted over time. Your dog might learn to ignore the sound of the click, as there's nothing in it for her.

The "hot zone" is the spot right next to your body where your dog gets paid with a treat.

side, and good treats like store-bought biscuits when she's not pulling but also not walking close to you.) Initially, you want your dog to understand that the loose leash earns clicks and treats. After your dog learns that lesson, you can begin to refine the behavior by requiring her to walk closer to you, but that comes in time.

Continue walking and click-treating your dog for keeping the leash loose. When you give your dog the treat, hand it over in such a way that she has to come near you in order to collect it—don't reach out to give it to your dog where's she's standing a few steps away from you. You want your dog to understand that the "hot zone," where all the good stuff happens, is right next to your leg. If your dog opts to walk closely to you on the side without the treats, you should still acknowledge it with a click but then show her that you have the treat in the hot zone on the other side of your body so that she scoots around to get it on the proper side. With consistent reinforcement in that spot—the spot where she gets all of the treats—she'll start *choosing* to hang out in the area. This is a small modification in the leash-training routine that reaps great rewards.

Be generous with your clicks and treats during the early stages of the process. Every time you click you're giving your dog valuable information about what "works." At the same time you're learning to watch your dog closely. Rather than tuning out during a walk and letting your dog drag you down the street, you're forced to tune *into* her and really connect with her. Look for all of the small but click-worthy behaviors that tell your dog that she's "getting warmer," like looking up at you, slowing down to match her pace to yours, arcing toward you, and looking away from distractions like other dogs. Each time you click these types of behaviors you're telling your dog, "I like this, keep it up!" Your dog, on the other hand, might think, "This is simple!"

It's easy to fall into a rhythm as you walk, where you click every eight steps, or every block, or every time your dog speeds up and then slows down to walk near you. The problem is that dogs pick up on patterns very quickly, so your dog might realize, "I can do whatever the heck I want during these walks as long as I veer back to my person when we hit the end of the block." You should strive to click when your dog deserves it, not just because you've fallen into a pattern of step-step-step-click-treat. If your dog is working hard to match your pace and is walking somewhat close to you with a loose leash, you should be a click-treating machine.

When your dog is reliably walking without pulling, it's time to start the first phase of the treat-weaning process. How quickly you and your dog get to this stage depends on a number of factors. If your dog has been pulling successfully for years, it's likely that it will take you longer to help your dog understand the new rules of the game. If you walk your dog only a few times a week, you might find that the "newness" of the environment each time you go out will make it difficult for your dog to focus on you instead of the surroundings. Similarly, if you aren't consistent about training every single time you take a walk, your dog will take longer to understand that pulling *never* works.

Refining the behavior: Initially, all your dog needs to do is walk with some slack in the leash in order to earn click-treats. But wait, there's more! When your dog has mastered the basic "walk-without-pulling" technique (for which you've been very, very generous), make her work a little harder to earn the clicks. If she opts to walk with slack in the leash but a few feet away from you, praise her for a job well done, but refrain from clicking until she swings in closer to your leg. If she understands that she needs to keep her body close to yours as you walk, require that she walks in that position for a longer period of time before she earns a click treat. You can raise your criteria for click-worthy behavior in a number of ways. You can require that your dog walks right by your side instead of a few steps ahead or behind (you're focusing on her positioning), you can ask her to walk near you for longer periods of time before you click (you're focusing on the duration of the behavior), and you can capture those moments when she looks up at you and away from distractions on the horizon (you're acknowledging her attentiveness). After you start really observing your dog's behavior while out leash walking, you'll notice the many little things she's doing right in order to earn a click!

Being more selective about what you click is the first step in weaning off of the clicker and treats. After being rewarded generously during the initial phase of the process, your dog should now understand what "works" and should be offering proper behaviors regularly. It would be impossible to keep rewarding your dog with that level of frequency (plus it would be pretty fattening!), so when you and your dog have reached a reliable baseline, begin to reward the best examples of her leash-walking behavior. Rewarding her every so often, or using "intermittent reinforcement," is one of the most effective ways to strengthen a behavior. For example, gamblers are motivated to sit at a slot machine pulling the lever for hours in the hopes that the elusive payout is just one pull away. Dogs have a similar gambling instinct in that they will continue to play the game as long as they think that a treat might materialize.

As you become more selective about what you click—which means that your dog is "getting it"—you can also begin to wean off of the clicker. The clicker is an excellent tool when you're beginning leash training because of the clarity it provides, but when your dog has the hang of leash walking, you can use a less precise marker when you reward her, a click word like "yup." Say your click word when you would normally click, and then immediately follow up with a treat as always. Initially, the word won't have the same impact that the clicker has, but with consistency you should get that same head-snapping reaction when you say it.

What if my dog pulls anyway? It's wishful thinking to believe that once you begin leash training your dog will never pull again. The world is filled with temptations, so even though you have a pocket full of savory

Acknowledging Attention

It's a really big deal when your dog looks up at you during a walk. Not only is she ignoring the great big world around her, she's also looking to you as if to say, "We're in this together, right?" If you're otherwise engaged, like using the phone, you're going to miss these small but impactful moments, so when you walk, do so mindfully. Acknowledge your dog for looking up at your with a click and treat during the early stages of the process, and then warmly praise for her attention once you've weaned off the treats.

Dogs pull because it works. They pull, we follow!

treats, it's almost guaranteed that you'll eventually be trumped by a retreating squirrel, another dog, or a friendly stranger. Sometimes even the promise of a distraction is enough to make a dog pull; I've worked with dogs that hit a certain part of town and kick into turbo gear because they remember finding a tipped garbage smorgasbord there months before. So what should you do when your dog goes into a full-tilt pull?

First, your dog must learn that pulling isn't a viable strategy. Dogs pull because it works for them; they pull and we follow. This lesson is reinforced quickly, and before you know it you've got a dog that pulls because it gets her where she needs to go. Once you begin leash training, pulling should have the opposite effect. When your dog pulls, the walk comes to a *complete stop.* That means that the second the leash goes taut, you should stop immediately. This is a difficult step because most of us are used to tuning out and just holding on during walks. This part of leash training means that you can't talk on the phone and let your dog pull for twenty steps before you realize it! Being mindful during leash walks will not only enable you to prevent pulling, but if you're observant, it will also allow you to predict it before it begins. Dogs telegraph their intent though their bodies. When your dog takes several rapid steps ahead of you, it's likely that those quick steps are going to turn into a pull. Rather than continue walking and letting your dog's inertia pull you along, stop walking before your dog hits the end of the leash. The intent is not to jerk your dog off her feet when she hits the end of the leash, but to prevent further pulling.

Dogs usually do one of two behaviors when the walk abruptly stops. First, the dog might turn back to look at you as if to say, "What's going

Leash Pulling and the Sniffing Dog

Some scent-hungry dogs don't care if you come to a dead stop in response to their pulling. They'll happily stand still and sniff the grassy patch next to them, or even sniff the air, and the cessation of movement won't be the mild punishment you intend. If you stop when your dog pulls and she buries her nose in the neighbor's yard, oblivious that she's no longer moving, take a few steps away from the distracting area so that she can't continue to engage in the behavior. This will enable her to refocus on the walk instead of putting her energies into sniffing.

on?!" If your dog breaks focus from the open road ahead and glances at you, capture that moment with the clicker. Even though a look back doesn't seem like much to celebrate, it's an important building block, and it allows your dog to be "right" more quickly (and prevents frustration on both ends of the leash). Offer your dog her payment in the "hot zone" instead of reaching out to give the treat to her. By doing so, your dog will be back in the proper position near you when she collects her treat, and you can continue your walk "on the right paw," clicking and treating your dog for being close as you resume.

If you come to a stop and your dog continues pulling even though you're standing still, it's time for a more obvious indicator that pulling isn't an option: a "penalty yard." A penalty yard is a mild dog-safe punishment that teaches your dog that when she pulls, she actually loses ground instead of making forward progress. This technique works particularly well when your dog is pulling toward something tangible on the horizon, like garbage on the street or a friend down the block. The process is simple, and when executed properly, it provides a crystal-clear message to your dog that pulling doesn't work.

When your dog pulls, stop immediately and give her about two seconds to see if she's going to turn back to you on her own, as described above. If the focused dog isn't able to tear herself away from the distraction, drive home the point that pulling won't get your dog where she wants to go by walking backwards with her so that it's obvious she's losing ground. Don't turn around and walk away with your dog; a penalty yard requires that both you and your dog *back away* from the distraction ahead of you. Turning around could mean that you're a fickle leash walker and you just want to go in a different direction, while walking backwards keeps the temptation in your dog's sightlines as you both move farther away from it. You want your dog to realize that the distraction is still there but that pulling isn't going to allow her to reach it. This entire process should happen quickly and fluidly. Begin walking backwards at a steady pace immediately after the two-second count, so it's clear that the backwards movement is directly related to her pulling. You don't want your dog to go into a "sit" when she pulls, as this breaks up the cadence of the walk. The penalty yard should look like a quick dance with your dog.

Continue walking backwards with your dog until she manages to break her focus from the distraction ahead of her in order to look at you as if to say, "What's going on?" Sometimes it only takes a few backward steps before your dog redirects her attention to you, but often it can take upwards of five to ten steps. (Did I mention that doing penalty yards in public is embarrassing?) Once again, click to mark that magic moment when she looks back at you, and offer her the treat in the hot zone next to your leg. If your dog is faced with a tangible distraction, like a food wrapper, it's likely that she will collect her treat and then take off towards it once you start walking forward again. Repeat the penalty yard until your dog looks back at you, and continue to engage this way until your dog finally realizes that pulling isn't working to get her closer to her goal. It might take several repetitions before your dog understands that pulling on the leash is making the goal move farther away from her instead of closer to her, which means that you'll have to cover the same piece of real estate on the sidewalk a few times. Does it feel silly? Yes. Is it effective? *Yes.*

Some dogs balk and fight against the leash when you attempt a penalty yard. It's not a good idea to turn this simple training process into a tug of war, so instead of struggling with your dog to walk backwards, stop in your tracks. Your dog will probably remain fixed on the horizon, but don't allow her to pull forward. Wait a few moments and then attempt to put some slack in the leash by reaching your leash-holding hand forward a bit. If your dog feels the slack and tries to take off, don't move. If you slacken the leash and she manages to stay still, begin walking. If she goes right back to pulling, stop again. This method isn't as efficient as doing a penalty yard, but it does drive home the point that the walk stops when the leash is tight, and commences when there's slack in it.

If you consistently do either the quick stop when your dog pulls or the penalty yard, your dog will begin to "self-correct" right after the leash goes tight, meaning your dog will feel the tension in the leash and seem to say, "Ooh, pulling is no longer an option for me. I need to circle back to my person so we can keep moving forward!" Even the best-trained dog can occasionally lose her head for a moment and attempt to pull while on leash. The dog that has learned that a tight leash means *stop* also knows how to make the walk commence by heading back to her person. A penalty yard with a leash-savvy dog will decrease from multiple steps backwards to requiring just a half step back. With a well-versed dog, the process becomes

> ## New Horizons
>
> Once your dog understands basic leash manners in your everyday environment, bring her to new neighborhoods to test her skills. Although she might have all the right moves during her daily walks, bringing her to a new location might require a quick behavioral "reboot." Dogs don't generalize well, so don't be surprised when your newly rehabilitated puller resorts to her old habits when you visit a different street. Be prepared to go back to the basics every time you take a new route, but recognize that your dog will probably fall in line much more quickly because of all of your prior hard work!

quick and elegant, where the dog pulls forward, you pause for a moment to prevent further pulling, and she circles back to your side almost immediately.

Dogs that refuse treats: My techniques for pull-free walks are treat-heavy, but what should you do if your dog refuses treats while out for a walk? Does that mean you're destined for a lifetime of pulling?

First, take another look at the treats you're using. Although your dog might adore peanut butter biscuits around the house, they might not be enticing enough to trump her natural inclination to pull during your average walk. If your dog turns up her nose at your walk treats, upgrade to something irresistible, like little pieces of cheese or chicken. Consider how you feel about graham crackers and chocolate cake; they're both desserts, but one is much more enticing than the other! Once you begin refining your dog's leash-walking skills, you can extend the weaning process to the types of treats you're offering. Keep a stash of the extra-special treats along with biscuits and some of her daily kibble ration so that she never knows what she's going to get. It's doggie trail mix!

If you're already using a top-notch treat that you know your dog adores and she's still refusing it, she might be overstimulated or nervous in the environment. When I first brought our boxer Sumner home at a year old, he was scared and reactive during our walks around the neighborhood. I stuffed my pockets full of treats that he nearly always turned down. Even though the treats weren't having their desired impact I wasn't willing to give up and let him pull me down the street, so I used a combination of techniques to quell his ingrained pulling habit. Every time he pulled, I stopped and waited for a few seconds to see if he would turn to look at me. Sometimes he did, to which I praised him and continued walking. He quickly learned to self-correct and come back to my side when I stopped walking, and even though he refused the treats I offered him, the promise of continuing with the walk was reward enough. I also had to do many penalty yards with him, and he responded to them without treats as well. We did our daily walks without the benefit of treats for many months, and those two simple techniques—stopping when he pulled and doing a penalty yard if necessary—paved the way for years of polite walking. In time I was able to introduce treats to help deal with his leash reactivity (more on that in Chapter 10), and my nervous pulling dog became a model leash walker.

When Is Leash Training "Done"?

Keep in mind that leash training is a marathon behavior, so being "done" with it will come gradually. Leash-walking manners happen, literally, a step at a time. It's a good idea to keep treats in your pocket even after your dog is trotting by your side during most of the walk, as the unexpected payout will help to keep your canine gambler in the game. Even though Millie and Olive are good leash walkers, I still pocket a few small treats when we walk for those moments when they glance up at me or maintain a nice long stretch of "hot zone" walking. I'm not reinforcing them at the same rate I did when they were first figuring out polite walking, but the occasional well-timed goody helps to remind them that they never know when they're going to get "paid."

There is no official leash-walking code of conduct, and I'll admit that I'm not a stickler when it comes to leash-walking manners. My requests are that the dog at the other end of the leash can walk without pulling

Beyond Treats

Many dogs are motivated by food rewards, but not all are adequately aroused by the promise of a treat. It's important to give some thought to your dog's unique motivators before you engage in any training exercise. (Keep in mind the hierarchy of food rewards; a dry biscuit rates far below a piece of cheese or chicken.) While treats are the most convenient rewards to use because of their variety and ease of dispensing, play can be a major motivator for those dogs not adequately moved by food. When leash walking a play-crazy dog, bring a small tug toy or a ball on a rope in your pocket. Keep it hidden to stop the play-crazy dog from fixating on it instead of the walk and to prevent it from turning into a bribe. Offer the toy to your dog after a stretch of polite walking; mark the behavior with your clicker or click word, and then engage in a quick game of tug or short-distance fetch. Ask your dog to drop the toy, and then put it away and resume your walk. Finding the right motivator for your dog can mean the difference between a lackluster response and a stellar one.

(preferably close to me), that she picks one side of my body to walk near and doesn't zigzag in front of me, and if she loses her head for a moment and does pull, that she will quickly self-correct and loosen the leash. Those seemingly simple criteria can take time to hone, but once you get there, you and your dog will enjoy a future of peaceful, easy leash walks!

eight

TRAINING PROBLEM TWO: RUNNING AWAY

Coming when called is simple in theory: you say "come" and your dog races to you. The reality is that this cue is one of the more challenging behaviors to perfect because of environmental competition, like interesting smells and other people and dogs, and a lack of well-rounded practice. Many of us go through basic training and get lulled into a false sense of security that our dog really understands what we mean when we say "come" because most dogs respond readily in a predictable environment. The first time you try to get your dog to come when she's in the park playing with friends or faced with a field of scent trails, however, you'll discover that the word "come" might not have the same impact. What's more, your dog might realize that she doesn't *have* to come—four legs trump two, so if she's off leash there's a good chance that your attempts to get your dog to come to you will end up a game of "catch me if you can." The good news is that the fundamentals of teaching a speedy recall are simple, and even the most recall-resistant dogs can learn that coming when called can be a fun game.

Case Study: Rebecca adopted her dog Angus from Corgi rescue when he was six months old. The young dog had been found as a stray, but it was clear that he had once lived in a home. He scratched at the door without prompting when he wanted to go out for a potty break, and he knew how to sit when asked and drop the ball when playing fetch. Rebecca worked with a private obedience trainer and discovered just how clever her new dog was. Angus picked up all of the basic training cues quickly, from "down" to "stay" to a few cute tricks. The one cue Angus never quite got the hang of, though, was coming when called. His response was always good when they were in a training scenario in the house—Angus would come running when they were playing the predictable "recall game," but Rebecca couldn't count on him to come reliably when she called him in real-life scenarios.

Rebecca stopped giving Angus treats for coming when called after a few weeks of practicing it around the house, assuming that he knew how to do it in every situation. Even though he wasn't even close to being reliable when she called him to come in from the yard, she felt that she had done enough treat training with him, and that he should come to her because he knew what was expected of him. In time, Angus's once semireliable recall quickly became a full-fledged blow-off, which frustrated Rebecca. She reacted by yelling at Angus when he wouldn't come, chasing him to try to grab him, and scolding him when she finally got her hands on him. While Angus was nearly perfect at all of his other obedience cues, his lack of recall was enough to make Rebecca think she had a very naughty dog indeed.

Possible Outcome One: Rebecca's morning routine was to feed Angus and then let him play in the fenced yard while she got ready for work. Angus enjoyed being outside and was reluctant to come back in when it was time for Rebecca to leave. Rebecca called Angus with increasing urgency as the minutes ticked by. Though she was once able to bribe him by shaking a box of dog treats, the clever pup soon figured out that he could grab the treat Rebecca offered him and dash just out of her reach. What was once a five-minute inconvenience stretched into a half-hour exercise in frustration. Rebecca felt bad about leaving him alone for most of the day, so Angus's morning yard idyll was fueled by guilt. She refused to deny him his time outside. On the mornings when she was quick enough to get her hands on him, she scolded Angus for blowing her off as she carried him inside. She spent many a cold, rainy morning standing on her small porch, varying from cajoling to demanding that Angus come in. Her departure time for work inched later, until her supervisor commented on her tardiness with disapproval. Rebecca couldn't believe that her *dog* was getting her in trouble at work.

Possible Outcome Two: Rebecca knew that Angus was unreliable off leash because he rarely came when she called him, so she always made sure to leash him up any time they left the house. Her management plan worked well until the day Angus was startled by a backfiring car during a walk and he slipped out of his collar. Rebecca knew that she was in a dangerous situation—the sidewalk they were on was near a busy street—so she called to him sharply. Angus froze, almost as if he recognized the tension in Rebecca's voice. She took a few tentative steps toward him, and Angus understood that Rebecca was gearing up for a game of "you can't catch me." He darted a few steps out of her reach. Rebecca, now scared and angry, called to Angus while she ran toward him. The young dog had always enjoyed being chased, so he took off down the sidewalk, deftly avoiding the other people trying to grab him. Angus disappeared around a corner with Rebecca trailing far behind, calling, "Angus, come!" over and

Dog on the Loose

Trying to capture a loose dog is a stressful situation, particularly when near busy streets. What could Rebecca have done differently to get Angus back safely? She was initially in a good position to recapture him because Angus didn't take off running without looking back; he remained close to her and watched her. Instead of chasing after him, Rebecca should have gotten his attention and run in the *opposite* direction. Most dogs can't resist rapidly retreating objects, so it's likely Angus would have chased after Rebecca as if playing a game. She could have run to a safer spot and crouched down so that Angus could approach her, allowing her to slowly reach for him to pet him, and then gently take hold of his collar. Talking softly to dogs in scenarios like this one helps to reduce the tension of the moment as well. It's not easy to quell the instinct to dash after a loose dog, but unless you're an Olympic sprinter, it's unlikely that you'll be able to grab your dog by chasing it.

over. As she chased him down the street, Rebecca wondered if this was how he had ended up homeless in the first place.

Angus was a perfectly trained dog in all other aspects but his recall. Rebecca's frustration with him fueled the problem, as Angus didn't want to approach her when she was yelling at him. What could this duo have done to avoid the tension surrounding a straightforward cue?

The Rules of the Recall

While the basic behavior is simple to teach, the recall is a rule-bound cue—there are some definite *dos* and *don'ts* when starting out. Mastering these simple rules will enable you to improve your dog's recall quickly, and will help to avoid typical "newbie" pitfalls.

- **Pick a special word:** Many of us use a hybrid of our dog's name and "come, come, come" when we call our dogs. If you've been getting less than stellar results when using these recall words, meaning your dog ignores you when you say them, quit using them. If you're just starting out training a new dog, pick a word other than her name; it's likely that you say your dog's name more often than you think, which means it can become verbal wallpaper. (That's the reason I rarely say my canine clients' names—I'll use "sweetie" or "cutie" unless I *really* need the dog to focus on me.) You want to use a word that's special, and more specifically, a word that doesn't have "I-don't-have-to-listen" baggage associated with it. I use the word "here" because most dogs haven't been exposed to it. You can use any word at all, just be consistent about it.

- **Use a happy tone of voice:** This step usually comes naturally to women, but it's tougher for men because of their deeper voices. It's not necessary to sing your recall word, but do strive to sound upbeat when you say it. Again, you want your dog to understand that this is a fun game, and you're excited to be playing it with her!
- **Say your recall word only once:** This is probably the most difficult rule to put into practice. (I often joke with my clients that I should have it tattooed on my forehead as a reminder!) Although we expect instant results in so many aspects of our lives thanks to technology, we need to remember that our dogs are not computers! It takes a few moments for the word "here" to come out, for the sound to travel to our dog, for our dog to process what "here" means, and then react appropriately. Saying the word over and over again won't make your dog come to you faster, but it might make your dog learn that you don't really mean it until you've said it five times! I've found that saying the word once and then following up with a whistle or kissy noise can help speed the process and help your dog understand what she needs to do. Once your dog has mastered the basic recall concept you can wean the ancillary noises and just rely on the word itself. (Even though my dogs know how to come when called, I still whistle and clap my hands to encourage a speedy response.)
- **Watch your body positioning:** I've worked on the Animal Planet TV show *Puppy Bowl* for the past eight years. The show is broadcast on Super Bowl Sunday, and it features groups of adorable rescue pups playing on a scaled-down football field. One of my responsibilities as the behind-the-scenes puppy wrangler is to coax the untrained puppies to run out of a small chute and onto the field one at a time for their "player introductions." The field is brightly lit and surrounded by cameras and people, so when the dog first peeks her head out of the chute, it's quite an overwhelming sight. I'm positioned on the field directly across from the chute, so when the puppies dash across the field, they come running to me in such a way that all four cameras shooting can capture the dash. Although it probably looks ridiculous to the rest of the crew, I *lie down* on the field so that my body position is completely nonthreatening to the puppies, since everything else surrounding them looks pretty scary! My low nonthreatening position coupled with my happy calls are usually enough to get these nervous pups to cross the field. Now, I'm not suggesting that you need to lie flat on the ground in order to get your dog to come to you, but I am saying that getting low and sitting on the floor or kneeling will

encourage a speedier response during the initial teaching phase. Once your dog has a grasp of the basics, you can begin to stand tall.

- **Praise accordingly:** Learning how to come when called is a *huge* deal. It can mean the difference between life or death in some scenarios (like in Angus's case), so it's important to acknowledge your dog's responses with the appropriate amount of fanfare. Praise your dog the second she turns to look at you after you call her, and then continue to praise her as she races to you. Keep praising her once she reaches you. You want your dog to think that she's a genius for what she just did! A word of caution: watch your dog's response when you praise her for coming to you. If you reach out to pet her and she dashes away, you're actually teaching her to avoid you! Try to stick with verbal praise and an appropriately delicious goody instead of doing a lot of hands-on rewarding.
- **Reward accordingly:** Make sure that the treat you're offering your dog each time you verbally praise her is worthy of the Herculean feat that she's accomplishing. Dry biscuits might cut it around the house and in familiar environments, but use a "sexier" treat when you start introducing new environments.
- **Keep your recall word sacred during the teaching phase:** The concept of "verbal wallpaper" also applies to your recall word. If you say it over and over, the word's impact and importance will slowly fade. Your dog's responses to your recall should be reflexive, meaning she hears the word and responds almost without thinking. (I liken this to what happens when the doctor hits your knee with that rubber mallet. You can't control your response, it just happens.) By "sacred" I mean that you refrain from saying the word until you're in a situation when you're 99 percent sure that your dog is going to respond to it, and you're 100 percent sure that you're ready to reward her for doing it. I catch my clients casually saying "here" to their dogs throughout our training sessions, sometimes rewarding their dogs for responding but more often than not, skipping the reward. I feel like the recall police when I have to tell them to knock it off! During the initial training period, keep the recall word on a high shelf and take it down only when you're really ready to use it!
- **Don't associate the recall word with anything negative:** If you say "here" and you consistently bring your dog into the house or leave the dog park, she will quickly learn that "here" means "the fun is ending." Practice your recall frequently when you *don't* need your dog to come to you, and release her to play after successfully completing it. That

way your dog will never know if she gets to play for another ten minutes, or if it's truly time to leave.

- **Don't test the recall before your dog is ready:** A lightning-fast recall is built incrementally over time. Much like any training cue, getting to a "proofed" behavior is like going from K to 12. You would never ask a kindergarten student to try to read a novel, much like you should never ask your dog that is just figuring out the recall to attempt a recall in an unfamiliar setting before she's ready. Dogs don't generalize well, so coming when called in your home or yard is vastly different from doing it in the park. Dogs that don't respond in unfamiliar settings aren't necessarily being "insubordinate"; often the dogs haven't learned what to do in a new environment.
- **Don't grant off-leash freedom until it is earned:** Unclipping the leash and letting your dog run free is a privilege that needs to be earned as a team. If you don't trust that your dog is going to come back to you when you call, why would you allow her off leash to "practice" the behavior?

Teaching a Basic Recall

After that exhaustive rule book, the good news is that the first step of teaching the basic recall couldn't be easier. Even though this training exercise seems rudimentary, you should use it whether you're working with a brand-new puppy or an adult with exposure to the recall.

Pick an open room in your home and then grab some high-value treats and a few helpers so that at least three people are playing the game. (Your recall practice sessions should be fun and should feel like a game!) Have everyone sit on the ground a short distance away from each other. Ask one player to say "here" in an upbeat, happy voice. I teach this first step as a learn-as-you-go cue, so that your dog can figure out how to do it on the fly instead of needing an intensive introductory period. The tone of your voice and your relaxed low posture should be enough context clues for your dog to understand what you're asking. When your dog hears the word, one of two things might happen. She might gleefully bound over to the person who called, at which time that person should click and hand over the meaty treat, and then praise generously. If your dog doesn't respond to the initial call, ask the person to whistle, clap their hands, or make kissy noises as an inducement. Ask the caller to praise your dog when she turns to look, and continue praising as she approaches. (Don't forget to have the caller get low to the ground and watch his or her body language if the dog seems reluctant to approach.) Continue this process with all of the players, switching turns and gradually moving farther apart so that the game doesn't

The Recall and the Bond

In my book *Bonding with Your Dog: A Trainer's Secret to Building a Better Relationship,* I describe how a missing recall can be a sign that something isn't quite right in a canine-human bond. Of course, there is a major training component to a strong recall, as evidenced in the contents of the next few pages, but taking a mindful look at the relationship you have with your dog might uncover some other reasons that your recall is "off." Have you punished your dog for not coming to you? Do you have to chase and grab at your dog in order to get her to come? Do you get angry at your dog when she doesn't come to you immediately? Reframing these possible reasons will help you work through pitfalls and repair any damage done.

become predictable for the dog. Keep the training sessions short and leave your dog wanting more. Play this game throughout the house over the course of several days, and then move to the next step: hide-and-seek.

The Hide-and-Seek Recall

The hide-and-seek recall takes the game from basic to better by introducing an element of surprise. Assemble your team of helpers and instead of standing in the same room, spread out throughout your home. The first person to call your dog should say "here" and follow up with some encouraging noises like whistling and clapping, since it won't be obvious to your dog where the person is hiding. As always, praise for the approach and reward the arrival with a treat (or a toy, if your dog is play motivated). Then ask the next person to call your dog. Each player should move to a new room after their turn, so the canine participant never knows where she should go next. Get creative with your hiding spots as your dog gets better at the game. Try hiding in closets or even in the shower!

By this time you want your dog *racing* to get from person to person. The recall game should be fun and unpredictable. This is an important foundation step, whether you're training a newbie or an older dog that has learned to blow off your requests to come when called. You want your dog to understand that coming to you when you call is not only highly rewarding (the treats or play), but it's also an interesting game. This training exercise is an excellent way to burn off your dog's excess energy when the weather is bad and you can't play outside, or when you have a punchy puppy that just won't settle down.

Olive gives the hide-and-seek recall a try.

Once your dog understands the hide-and-seek recall, try a few surprise sessions. Surreptitiously sneak out of the room, grab a treat, and call your dog. You should get an immediate and joyful response, as if your dog is thinking, "Now? We're doing this *now?*" Adding this unpredictable element will help your dog understand that you can make good things happen out of thin air, and she should keep an eye on you. In addition, this step will help your dog learn that the recall isn't always a part of a predictable Round Robin. Sometimes it happens out of the blue!

The Distraction Recall

By this point your dog should have a strong, almost reflexive response to the recall word. Now it's time to begin "proofing" the behavior by adding an element of distraction. Think about the things that typically attract your dog's attention. Is she interested in dirty socks? Wadded up paper towels? Does she steal Q-tips? Any distraction other than food is fine to use during the initial stages of this process. Ask your helper to present one of your dog's preferred distractions to her. Tell your helper to keep the item encased in her hands so that your dog can see it and sniff it but can't put her mouth on it or steal it. Let the dog interact with the item for a few moments, and then take a deep breath and say your recall word.

Now, it's possible that your dog won't respond to the word as reflexively as she has in the past because of the tempting sock/towel/Q-tip right in front

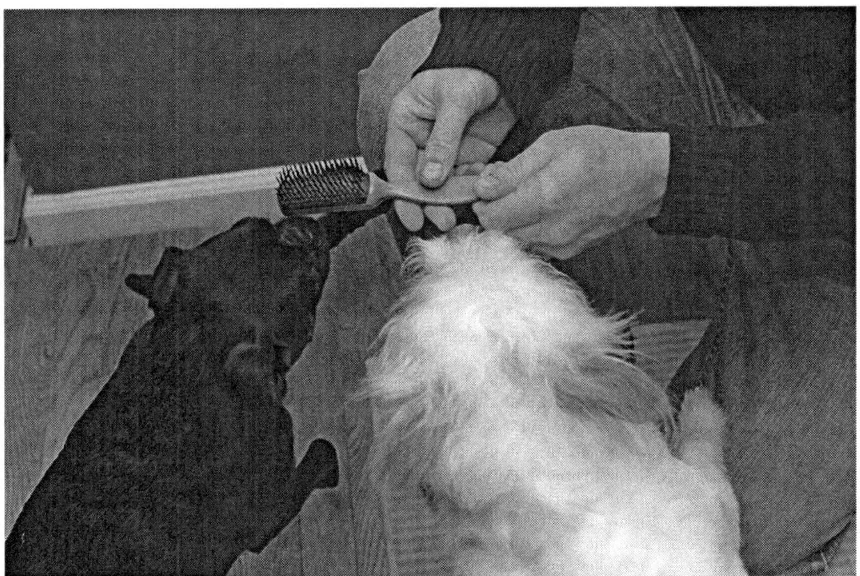

Even a hairbrush can be a distraction during the distraction recall game!

of her nose. It's okay! (If your dog *does* come to you immediately, have a party. It's a big deal.) Don't repeat the recall word, but instead try some of the same inducements you used when you were first teaching her to come when called, like whistling and clapping. If your dog manages to break focus from the distraction and look toward you, praise her! This shift in focus is the first step to getting a full-fledged response. If your dog is unable to look away from the distraction, consider using a less distracting distraction and then working up to the more difficult item. You want the distraction to be of interest to your dog, but not so much so that it completely trumps the treat you have to offer. Eventually, with practice, your dog should be able to come off all distractions in this controlled environment, but that level of responsiveness takes time and practice.

The goal of this exercise is to be able to present a variety of items your dog will be intrigued by, but that the moment she hears you say "here," she will abandon the item and run to you. It's not just the promise of the reward that should motivate her, though. Your rich history of fun successful recalls should create a dog that understands that no matter how intriguing a distraction is right in front of her nose, you're always the best game in town!

Moving Outside

Once you've done a variety of recalls in the house, it's time to move to the great outdoors. Even though your dog is a pro at her indoor recalls at this

Finding Safe Open Spaces

You don't have to be a land baron to practice outside recalls safely. Our first home had a tiny yard, so in addition to practicing in it, I also found creative outdoor practice spots. If you're lacking a fenced outdoor space, try:

- **Community tennis and basketball courts:** Yes, you might be bending the rules by bringing your dog in, but if you visit during the early morning or evening hours or during the off seasons, you'll be less likely to upset people. The rules on our neighborhood courts said "NO DOGS," but since no one ever used the courts I had no problem working with them there.
- **The local dog park:** This might sound like contradictory advice since I've said you should begin practicing in nondistracting environments, but if you visit the park during off-peak hours, you might have the entire space to yourself. Try going early in the morning, or right before the park is set to close. Allow your dog to get the lay of the land by exploring the smells before you attempt your first recall. Then once you're confident that he's had a chance to explore, get to work.
- **Fenced-in neighbors:** Ask your friends and neighbors if you can spend some time practicing in their fenced-in yard. Let them know that you won't need to spend hours practicing: even a half dozen recalls every few days will help.

point, everything changes once you hit grass (or pavement). Finding a dog-safe space in which to practice is critical. No matter how confident you are in your dog's burgeoning recall abilities, if you're still in the teaching or reteaching phase of the process, don't give your dog the opportunity to run away in an open field. You're competing with a multitude of new distractions outside, so you should stack the deck in your favor by going to a *familiar* or, at the very least, nondistracting fenced area to begin your outdoor practice.

Get your dog warmed up by doing a few basic recalls, where you just call her to you from a short distance away and then reward her. Let her wander around the open space. Watch for moments when she's not directly engaged with sniffing or exploring and call her to you again. Remember to reward with a very high value treat, and celebrate her responsiveness with praise. When your dog is a short distance away from you again, hide behind a tree and try it again. Toy-motivated dogs tend to do well when working on outside recalls, so bring a toy along if that's the case. If your dog is partial to fetch, call her to you, keeping the ball or toy hidden (remember, you shouldn't have to bribe your dog by showing her the toy to get her to come to you), and then the moment she reaches you, throw the toy for her. If your dog likes to play tug, offer her one end of the toy when she gets to you and have a good game of tug for a few minutes. (Does your dog know the rules of tug? Check out pages 51–53 for details.) Don't allow your dog to keep the reward toys post-recall, as controlling your dog's access to the reward toy will keep it special.

When working outside, throw in the occasional "run-away" recall. Call your dog to you, and when she looks at you, take off running in the opposite direction. Reward her when she catches up to you. This little twist on the typical recall makes it seem even more like a game, and it reminds your dog that you're fun and unpredictable.

If you find that your dog is slow to come to you when you call outside, or doesn't seem to want to come at all, consider switching to a better treat, or moving to a less distracting environment. Strive to avoid frustration during the early stages of outside recall training. A dog that has learned to ignore you when you call will be quick to pick up on any "recall static" like a strained tone of voice, which might make her even less likely to come to you. Remaining mindful will help. Remember that getting angry with your dog won't make her run to you any faster. It might just make her run *away* instead.

When Is Recall Training Done?

Much like every other training behavior, you're never "done" working on the recall. Coming when called needs to be practiced frequently in as many novel situations as possible to ensure that your dog always understands what the word "here" means. Similarly, for longer than you think necessary, you should continue to reward your dog for coming when called. If you consider how important the recall cue is—it keeps your dog safe, it demonstrates the bond that you have with one another, and it proves that you trump every other distraction around—it makes sense to pay your dog for successful recalls.

Once you're confident that your dog understands the recall concept and you've spent time practicing it, you don't have to reward every single recall with food. That said, you should at the very least give your dog *tons* of praise for coming when called. Even though you will naturally wean off treats over time, keep a few in your pocket so that you can reward her when she least expects it. This intermittent schedule of reinforcement is the best way to keep a behavior alive, because it taps into a dog's innate gambler. For example, you could call your dog to you from a short distance away and praise her, and then wait a few moments and call her to you again, offering her a treat when she arrives at your feet. Allow her to explore and then call her again, this time offering a toy that you had hidden in your pocket. Both of my dogs are excellent "recallers," and even though I can rely on their responses whether we're in our big new backyard or hiking off leash on a trail, I still offer treats or play when they don't expect it.

Coming when called can be frustrating prior to getting a handle on it, but it can turn into one of the most beautiful and impressive behaviors in your and your dog's repertoire if you take the time to work on it. If you take the tension out of the exercise, practice frequently, and reward heartily in a number of different ways, you'll end up with a dog that joyfully bounds to you when you call. That's about as good as it gets!

nine

TRAINING PROBLEM THREE: GROOMING AND HANDLING

Not every dog enjoys being touched, particularly when it comes to basic health-and-wellness procedures like brushing teeth and clipping nails. I experienced it firsthand when Olive growled at me to tell me that she did *not* want me wiping off her muddy paws. The two typical responses to this type of growl—telling the dog to stop it or backing away from the dog—do nothing to prevent the issue from festering. Dogs that refuse exploratory handling make it challenging for their people and their veterinarians and groomers to perform necessary wellness procedures, resulting in stress all around.

Case Study: Richard and Kerry brought Baron the Maltese home when he was fourteen weeks old. He came from a reputable breeder who believed in early socialization and handling, so Baron was a confident and appropriate puppy. The loved everything about their new dog, even the way that he playfully nipped at their hands when they tried to comb his coat. At first they laughed when he bared his teeth and growled at them when the comb came out, but they soon realized that Baron *really* didn't like being brushed. The pair knew that taking care of his coat in between grooming appointments was important, so they did their best to wrestle him into submission when it came time to brush him. Richard stood next to Baron and placed the dog's head under his arm so that Kerry could comb his coat from the shoulders down without getting nipped. When it came time to brush up near his face, Richard held the dog's head tightly between his hands as Kerry nervously reached out to brush him. The brushing was probably slightly uncomfortable for Baron, but the rituals surrounding the procedure only made the process that much more unbearable for him. They resorted to tricking him when they needed to groom him: Kerry would sneak a few strokes in when he was sleeping on the couch, only to have him wake with a startle, bark at her, and run away. He even became wary of walking near the bathroom where they kept the brush.

Possible Outcome One: Kerry and Richard began to notice that Baron no longer asked for petting when they sat on the couch together. When they

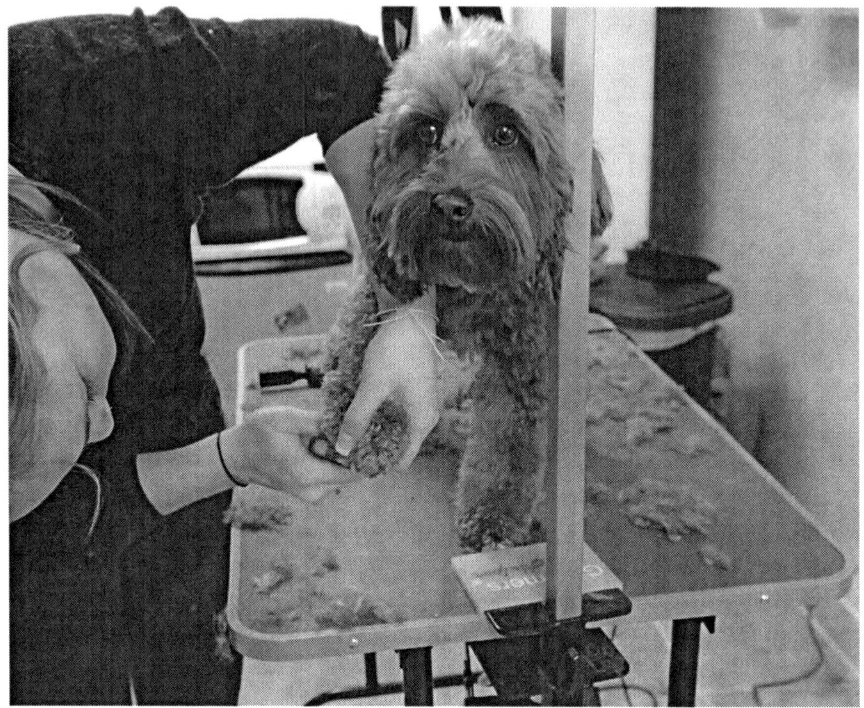

Nail trims don't have to be traumatic! Your groomer will thank you if you acclimate your dog to the process.

reached out to pet him the dog would duck his head away. When they did manage to get their hands on him Baron's body became stiff, as if he was tolerating the touch but not enjoying it. The moment they stopped petting him Baron would walk away, shaking off his body as if shaking them off. When it came time to leash Baron up for a walk, the dog ran from them even though he thoroughly enjoyed strolling outside. They often had to corner him in order to clip the leash to his collar. Baron became skeptical of any type of grooming equipment. There was no way that they could trim his nails, so they grew to floor-clicking length in between appointments. Brushing his teeth was out of the question as well, and Kerry and Richard hoped that the dental chews they gave Baron would prevent tooth issues in the future.

Possible Outcome Two: Baron's first trip to the groomer was stressful for everyone involved. They warned the groomer that Baron was "funny" about being brushed, but she assured them that she knew how to deal with it. When they picked Baron up hours later, he was panting and inconsolable. The grooming appointment had been a fight from beginning to end, and although the dog looked beautiful, they wondered at what cost.

Baron's trips to the groomer became more and more challenging. He put the brakes on the second he got out of the car at the salon, so Kerry had to drag him into the building. She knew that the groomer was gentle and kind, so she couldn't fault the woman for treating Baron poorly behind closed doors. It was clear that what had started off as a laughable behavior during puppyhood had morphed into a full-blown adult handicap.

Could Richard and Kerry have prevented Baron's extreme handling issues, or was the behavior cemented at an early age? Did they accidentally exacerbate Baron's reactivity? Let's rewind and consider some alternative handling possibilities.

Help Young Dogs Learn to Enjoy Handling

Teaching a puppy to tolerate, or in a perfect world *enjoy*, grooming and handling can be a fun process. Practice when your dog is tired but not punchy, meaning your dog is relaxed enough to allow you to explore her body without reacting like a typical goofy puppy. Arm yourself with a dry biscuit type of treat since a high-value treat might rev her up in this scenario. (We want her to enjoy the treat, but not be completely focused on it.) Envision all of the areas on your puppy's body that will need hands-on care. Begin by stroking your dog gently down her back and shoulders, and

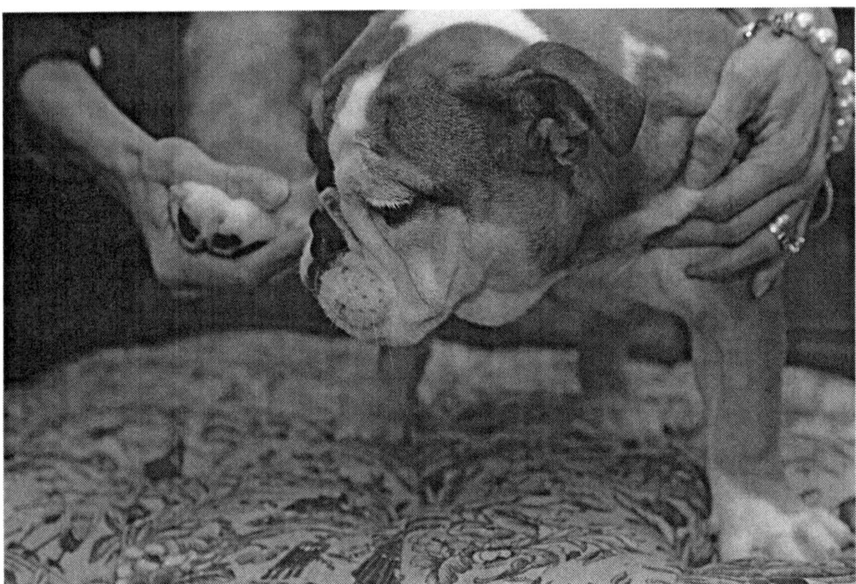

Helping your puppy to tolerate foot manipulation patiently helps with wiping paws and trimming nails.

then moving your hand down one of her front legs to her paw. Hold her paw in your palm for a moment, release, and then follow up with the biscuit. Repeat the process with her other front leg. Many dogs are wary about paw handling, particularly the back paws, so keep the initial rear-paw examination quick, and always reward with a treat. Work up to holding your dog's paw and examining it. Grasp it as you would to clip a nail, release, and follow up with a treat.

Introduce gentle ear exploration into your handling exercises. Get floppy-ear pups used to the sensation of having their ears turned over. Gently rub the bottom of the ear in your hands, and run your thumb along the edge of your dog's inner ear. Give your dog a treat for allowing the exploration. If you introduce this step at an early age and practice it frequently *before* you have to treat an ear infection, your dog will be much more likely to allow you to handle her ears, even if it's uncomfortable for her. For pointy-ear dogs, gently run your thumb along the exposed pink part of the ear. I've found that dogs that haven't developed a fear of ear handling actually enjoy the sensation of having the inside of the ear rubbed. Both of my dogs tilt their heads toward my hand and heave a contended sigh when they get a quick ear massage!

Get your puppy accustomed to having the area near his eyes touched as well, particularly if you have a wrinkly-faced breed like an English Bulldog that requires crevice wiping, or a dog with light-color fur that might need tear treatment. Use your thumb to gently swipe beneath each eye area, and follow up with a treat. A healing massage practitioner taught me that gently stroking this area releases endorphins, so this is yet another area that can become a pleasure for your dog.

Prepare your puppy for tooth brushing before you actually have to do it by dipping your finger in beef broth or coconut oil and running it along your puppy's gum line. Gently lift her flews (her lips), examine her teeth, and then follow up with a treat. I trained both of my dogs to hold still when I look in their mouths by saying, "May I look?" as I put my hand on their muzzles. It's my way of letting them know that I need them to be completely still for a few seconds while I explore inside their mouths. Though they occasionally fuss when they know I'm going to check their teeth, the moment I say the magic phrase, they stop moving and hold still until I finish and tell them, "Thank you!"

Prepare your puppy for rear-end inspection as well. Touch and hold her tail and then follow up with a treat. The fuzz-butt dogs often need wiping help post-potty (Olive is one of them), so get your dog used to the sensation of being held around her waist while you swipe a tissue across her rear. As always, follow up with a goody.

Introduce Grooming Equipment Slowly

It doesn't matter if you're dealing with a brand-new puppy or a rescue dog that's new to you; when it comes time to introduce your dog to grooming equipment, go slowly! As always, be mindful when you consider your tools, and plan ahead so that you're not trying to use them in a crisis scenario. It's likely that you're going to get some "feedback" from your dog if you absolutely *have* to use those nail clippers before you've had a chance to properly introduce them. If you take your time exposing your dog to things like brushes, nail clippers, and toothbrushes, it's likely that you'll be able to take care of some of the upkeep behaviors for free instead of outsourcing them to professionals!

Brush: The type of brush you use on your dog will have an impact on how your dog reacts to it, and your dog's coat type dictates the type of brush you should use. Of course, the harder the bristles, the more likely it is that your dog might feel uncomfortable. The first few times that you introduce the brush or comb that you intend to use on your dog, do so with the understanding that no real brushing or combing is going to take place. Initially, you just want your dog to get used to the feeling of the instrument on her body. Show the brush to your dog, allow her to examine it, place it on a nonthreatening part of her body for a moment (like her shoulder), and then follow up with a food reward. Work up to a few light strokes followed by rewards, and then wrap up the session. Gradually increase the length of time you use the brush on your dog, stopping frequently to give treats for good behavior.

Toothbrush: Brushing teeth should be the easiest husbandry procedure since it includes a flavored toothpaste (and who doesn't like chicken-flavored toothpaste?), but many dogs balk at the process because it requires some facial restraint. Rather than loading up the toothbrush, grabbing your dog's muzzle, and jumping right in, first help your dog get comfortable with the requisite face handling. Gently take your dog's muzzle in your hands, briefly lift her lip, and then follow up with a treat. Repeat the process a few times on both sides of her mouth so that your dog doesn't struggle when you examine her teeth. Now it's time to introduce the toothbrush. First, let your dog check out the brush. It's fine if she wants to put it in her mouth, but don't allow the brush to become a chew toy. Gently place your hand on your dog's muzzle as you normally would when brushing, touch the brush to your dog's teeth, and then follow up with a food reward. (Are you sensing a pattern yet?) Repeat the process on the other side of your dog's mouth and then on the front teeth. Each brush should be quick and drama-free. Once again, don't expect to get any real tooth brushing done the first few times that you work with the toothbrush. The goal is that your dog should never struggle at any point during the process.

Touch Test

Is your dog truly enjoying your touch? Try this test: pet your dog for five seconds and then stop. How does he react? Does he lean in for more or walk away? Most of us assume that *every* dog loves human contact *all* the time, but that's not always the case. Of course, our dog's responses to touch are situational. In times of stress or high arousal, like at the vet or dog park, many dogs don't seem to appreciate touch, particularly from someone they don't know well. I've also watched people pet their own dogs at the end of a training session (which is usually a brain-draining experience) not noticing that their dog is trying to move away. Worse yet, I've witnessed well-intentioned strangers "loving up" dogs that clearly want nothing to do with the person.

When I meet a friendly dog, I do a version of the test to gauge if he wants me to touch him; I kneel down so that the dog is approaching my side and wait to see if the dog comes close to me. If he does I massage gently on the shoulders for a few seconds and then stop. If the dog leans into me, or solicits more petting with a paw or nose nudge, I give more. If the dog doesn't ask for more petting or backs away, I stop. Instead of assuming that every dog likes to be touched no matter what, it helps to watch the dog to see if he is truly enjoying the experience. Our dogs very clearly show us how they feel with their bodies; we just need to be more willing to listen to what they're saying.

Nail clippers: Finally, we have nail clipping. Couple the fact that many dogs have foot-handling issues with the very real possibility that you can accidentally cut your dog's nail painfully short, and you've got a recipe for stress on both sides of the clipper. As with the other grooming exercises, keep in mind that you won't be trimming any nails initially. It's important to get your dog comfortable with the ancillary handling that goes along with nail trimming before you actually begin, as the paw squeezing can be as stressful as the cutting itself. To begin, grasp your dog's paw in your hand and then give her a treat. Repeat the process, but each successive time you pick up your dog's paw, do so in the same way that you will when you need to cut the nail. There's a difference between casual handling and the specific action required for a successful nail trim, so work up to grasping your dog's paw and isolating a single nail as you would when about to clip it. If possible, give the treat while your dog's paw is still in your hand. This part of the training process looks like an easy-to-follow flow chart on paper, but the reality is less cut and dry. Do your best to help your dog understand that the touching and grasping you're doing is the *predictor* of the treat.

Olive used to hate having her paws touched, but after working with her, she now handles it with ease.

When your dog is comfortable with you touching and handling all four of her paws (and you will know that she is because she won't try to pull her paws away when you manipulate them), it's time to bring out the nail clippers. First just touch the clipper to her paw and give your dog a treat. Then isolate a single nail, touch the clipper to it, and follow up with a treat. Whether you move on to actual clipping during the session depends on your dog's reactions. If it looks as though your dog is accepting the handling, you can attempt a single nail and then wrap up the nail-clipping session. No matter how wonderfully your dog is doing, don't try to bulldoze through all twenty nails in the first session! If your dog seems unsure about the process—meaning she tries to pull her paw out of your hand when things start to get "real"—continue working on the basic handling techniques. When you are ready to begin clipping, do only one or two nails at a time, and reward your dog for her gracious acceptance of the process.

How quickly you move through any of these handling exercises depends on your dog. Some easygoing dogs might take to the new equipment within a few quick sessions, while others with handling baggage might take longer. Dogs with actual handling intolerance that react with intensity can benefit from a more intensive "touch-for-a-treat" program, as described in the following section.

Trimming Tips

- **Keep contortions to a minimum:** My old arthritic boxer Sumner didn't mind nail trims, but his back feet were always challenging because I couldn't get to them without making him uncomfortable. I discovered that if I held his paw as a farrier does with a horse, meaning his foot was in my hand with the top of the paw facing the ground, I could trim them without a problem. Get creative so that both you and your dog remain relaxed during trims: try placing your dog on the landing of a staircase and sitting one step down from him during trim time, or if you have a small dog, put him up on a table while you trim.
- **Provide incentives:** If you've got a super-wiggly dog, bring him in front a sliding-glass door and smear the window with peanut butter at nose height so that he can clean it while you trim.
- **Finish with a smile:** I always do something fun with my dogs the moment the last nail is cut. I'll offer to take them on a walk before the last paw hits the ground, or I'll whip out a toy and go a few rounds. Doing something fun after every nail trim will help to keep them trouble-free!

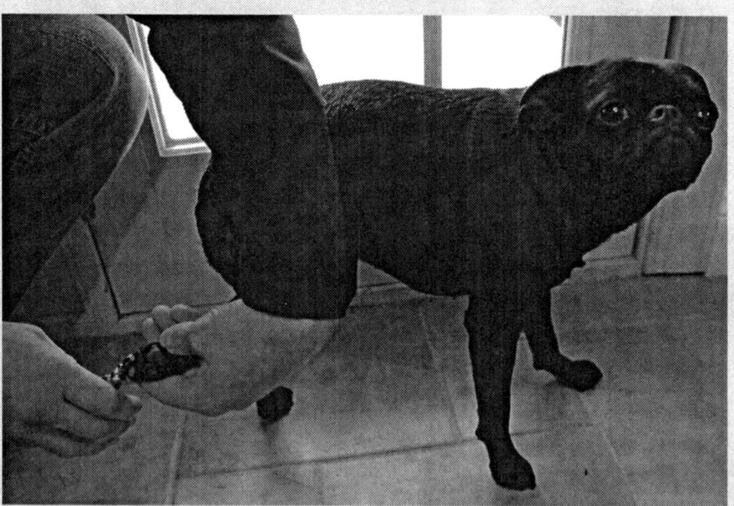

My dog Millie doesn't enjoy having her nails trimmed, but holding her back paws in this position helps to make it less uncomfortable for her.

Helping the Handling-Intolerant Dog

Some dogs come into their homes with fully formed handling issues that make any sort of care that involves touch—or for some even physical affection—challenging. The issues might be caused by a variety of reasons, from lack of early socialization to rough handling, but no matter the origin they can make routine care seem impossible. Dogs that feel uncomfortable about touch will show it in many ways, including:

- Attempting to move away
- Freezing
- Trembling
- Lip-lifting to show teeth
- Turning to look at person's hand or implement during touch
- Quickly orienting to person's hand or implement and placing mouth on it
- Biting (If you are concerned about biting, please seek qualified help rather than attempting this on your own.)

Before you begin working with your dog to help him overcome his handling sensitivities, it's important to first determine the areas of your dog's body that are the most tricky to touch. If you know that your dog dislikes having his feet touched more than any other part of his body, you'll want to begin working on an area that's in the same neighborhood, like the shoulders, but not at the exact epicenter of sensitivity. As always, grab a handful of moist, high-value treats like cheese or bits of lunch meat and keep them out of sight. Although this section addresses desensitizing ears to touch, this protocol can be used on any body part.

1. Reach toward the side of your dog's neck with the outside of your hand facing your dog (your palm should be facing you and your hand should be relaxed), and stop a few inches away from actually touching him. Feed him a treat with your other hand. Repeat the process a few times, watching to make sure your dog isn't becoming uncomfortable at this early stage. You want to see your dog anticipating the treat when you reach toward him (like licking his lips or looking at your hand that delivers the treats), as if he understands that the movement near his neck predicts a treat. Pause in between touches, and try not to work in a rhythmic pattern. (Dogs are excellent at picking up patterns.) Keep these initial sessions short—no more than two to three minutes—and wrap it up before your dog begins showing signs of stress. If you're progressing slowly, you shouldn't see your dog exhibiting any discomfort.

2. In the next session, work up to actually touching your dog on the neck with your hand and then feeding the treat with the other hand. Vary the rate at which you approach with the touching hand and where exactly you're touching him on his neck (keeping in mind that you don't want to get too close to his ears during the initial sessions). Again, look for your dog's anticipatory glance toward your treat-feeding hand after the touch, which means that your dog is beginning to pair the touch with the treat.
3. Once your dog is accepting touches of varying intensity and location on his neck, delay giving him the treat for a few seconds while you touch him. You want your dog to remain relaxed and accepting at this point so that you can move on to the more challenging steps.
4. In a new training session on a different day, begin the process from the first step, this time reaching out to the hot zone—your dog's ear. Reach toward it with your palm facing you and stop short of actually touching it. Feed with the opposite hand. Work through the rest of the steps slowly, varying the speed and direction at which you approach, over the course of days if necessary, to ensure that you're never pushing your dog out of his comfort zone.
5. Follow the same steps listed above until you are able to touch your dog's ear gently, and your dog shows signs that he knows a treat is coming. Remember that ear care requires more than just a gentle touch, though. Use the "touch-for-a-treat" method to get your dog comfortable with you folding the ear back, massaging the flap, inspecting the inner ear, and using a wipe to clean it. If your dog is worried about wipes or other objects near his ear like an ointment tube or drops, work through the same series listed above, but this time include the tool in your hand as you touch for a treat. Take your time working up to actually using the tool or applying the ointment, and make sure to reward generously with an extra-high-value treat the first time you use it.
6. Finally, help your dog understand that sometimes touches happen when he least expects it. Approach your dog and do a quick ear touch and reward him with a treat that was hidden in your pocket. Generalizing this behavior, or helping him understand that *all* ear touches are nonthreatening, is the final step.

Working with touch-sensitive dogs can be a slow process, so be patient! Allowing your dog to set the pace for this type of work, which requires a great deal of trust on the dog's part, will strengthen your bond with your dog, and eventually allow you to perform all of the necessary behaviors to keep your dog healthy and happy. It's a much better life for both of you when basic care procedures like ear, eye, and nail care are stress-free!

part three

BEYOND THE BASICS

ten

LEASH REACTIVITY

Sharing your home with a leash-reactive dog can bring a mix of frustration, embarrassment, and, in some cases, even fear. A dog that reacts explosively to outside stimulus, whether it's another dog or people or cars, turns what should be a leisurely stroll into a literal run through the gauntlet. Rather than enjoying walks, many leash-reactive dog guardians find themselves on watch from the moment they step out the door, always on alert for what might be coming around the corner. I speak from experience, as my boxer Sumner's deeply rooted reactivity tested me, but ultimately made me a more empathetic trainer. I lived with many of the same challenges my clients faced and worked through the ebb and flow of the training process on every single walk during the early days.

Case Study: Annie adopted Jax the light brown mixed-breed dog when he was about a year old. The rescue group didn't know anything about his background, and because they were at capacity with their foster families, they were eager to get him adopted out as quickly as possible. Annie was a novice dog owner who had only had a family pet growing up, but she fell in love with Jax's loving temperament at an adoption meet-and-greet and adopted him soon after.

Annie wanted Jax to be a part of her life and accompany her to as many places as possible. The first time she took him with her to run errands in her small town, he barked at a dog passing by across the street, but she chalked it up to a fluke. Jax had recently played with her friend's dog in their fenced yard, and the two dogs seemed to get along well. Over time, though, Annie noticed that Jax's reaction to other dogs during walks wasn't a fluke—it was constant. Every time they saw a dog while on a leash walk, Jax barked and lunged at the other dog with such intensity that it scared Annie. She had believed that her dog had a sweet temperament, but the Jekyll & Hyde personality change during walks always made her rethink how well she actually understood her new dog.

Jax's displays during walks made the two of them the talk of the town. People branded Jax the "mean dog" and gave them a wide berth. People who wanted to let their dogs meet Jax but hadn't encountered him before could barely ask, "Is your dog friendly?" before he began snarling. Annie started taking Jax for walks during the early morning hours before her neighbors were up and well after everyone had done their post-dinner dog walks. She was sad that her new best friend couldn't greet the world as happily as the other dogs she saw around town.

Possible Outcome One: Annie hopes that Jax will grow out of his anti-social behavior. She doesn't know what to do about his reactivity so she does nothing to work on it. He continues to be aggressive with every dog they pass. Over time his reactions become so intense that they frighten Annie, and holding on to him becomes more and more challenging. One evening when Annie was texting someone during their walk, Jax spotted a small white dog ahead of them. Jax barked and lunged and the leash slipped from Annie's hands. She watched helplessly as Jax ran up to the small dog and circled around it, barking and snarling as the owner tried to pick it up. "Your dog bit my dog!" the other owner screamed as she searched her small dog's body for wounds while Jax leapt at them. Thankfully the little white dog wore a coating of Jax's saliva but had no visible cuts. "I'm reporting your dog!" the other woman yelled. "He's vicious! I'm reporting him!" Annie wasn't sure what the outcome of the "reporting" would be, or what governing body would seek Jax out for his crime, but she spent the following few weeks in fear every time her home phone rang.

Possible Outcome Two: Annie hires a trainer to help her deal with Jax's reactivity on leash. He's expensive, but the reviews and photos of satisfied customers on his website make her feel confident that he knows what he's doing. At the first lesson he slips a metal choke collar over Jax's head and corrects him for lunging at another dog by "hanging" him from the leash so that the dog's front paws are off the ground. He repeats the process a few times, and Jax eliminates all over himself. Jax seems terrified, but Annie feels powerless to speak up against the "expert" who never stops talking as they walk. The trainer hands the leash to Annie and she tries to deliver a correction to Jax but feels terrible about it. That coupled with her slight stature makes it impossible for her to perform the correction properly. The trainer takes the collar off (and Jax attempts to bite him as he does it) and puts on a electric collar. "It's not painful," the trainer assures her, "It's just a tap to get his attention." Each time Jax barked at a passing dog, the trainer twisted the dial on the control pad in his hand and Jax reacted with a high-pitched scream and jump but less barking at the other dog. Annie purchases the collar at the end of the session because she saw minor improvement, but she uses it infrequently. Alarmingly, she notices that when Jax isn't wearing the collar that he also barks and lunges at joggers and cyclists in the way he used to react only to dogs.

Are Leash-Reactive Dogs Vicious?

Leash reactivity does not mean that a dog is bad, vicious, or "dominant." Dogs that have aggressive outbursts while on leash might be dealing with a number of different emotional responses to other dogs or people, including fear, stress, and frustration. When a leashed dog tips over into uncontrollable barking and pulling, it's as if he's in a tunnel and nothing else exists but the stimulus across the street. Typical coping skills like distancing and avoiding the stimulus aren't always an option for the leashed dog on a walk, so a nervous or stressed dog with no other options will resort to reactivity. Many dogs refuse treats and ignore their people when deep in the throes of reactivity, and then have difficulty "coming down" after a display because of the stress that's flooded their system.

Because the dog guardian often seems invisible to the dog during an aggressive display, leash reactivity can start to feel personal after a while. "Why is my dog doing this to me? Why won't he listen to me?" we think. It's important to remember that your dog is *not* doing it on purpose. Your dog is operating under the influence of powerful emotions. In his dog-brain, the stimulus across the street is something negative that needs to go away as quickly as possible, and barking is an efficient way to increase his distance from the scary/distressing thing. The reaction is not about you or your relationship with your dog.

The goal is to change your dog's perception of what the stimulus across the street represents. The methods to do so are a combination of systematic desensitization and counterconditioning. Desensitization is just what it sounds like: gradually making the subject less sensitive to the stimulus. Initially, the scary thing—the target—should be seen at a distance to keep

Attitude Is Everything

Dealing with leash reactivity can make even the sunniest person feel grumpy, but your dog needs you to find a positive attitude as you work through exercises. In the past you might have grasped the leash tighter and held your breath when passing a target, and it's likely that your dog picked up on that tension. Your goal is to stay as loose and happy as possible to help your dog understand that encountering a target doesn't make *you* upset. I used to chat jovially with my reactive dog Sumner when we passed other dogs to keep myself in the right headspace. "Look at that silly puppy!" I'd say to him. "He's saying hello to you! Isn't he nice? What a handsome dog!" It felt silly initially, but over time it became reflexive to give a cheerful running commentary during our run-ins with other dogs.

your dog from reacting to it (more on that in a bit), and over time, as your dog learns to accept the target, his distance from it is gradually decreased. Counterconditioning is actually *changing* your dog's perception of the target, so instead of having a visceral negative response to it he learns to associate positive emotions with it.

Before You Begin: Tools

Obviously, the most important tool required for a leash walk is a leash, but not just any leash will do. I'm a stickler for fixed-length leashes for all dogs, but *especially* for surly dogs. Allowing a reactive dog to roam ahead of you on a retractable leash is a bad idea because it permits your dog to greet whatever is on the horizon before you do. Even if your dog is all bluster and no bite, it's still not fair to let him harass other dogs and passersby at close range while you try to reel him in. In addition, you'll need to be able to reward your dog frequently when you're working on reactivity, which means that your dog will have to be close to you in order to make that happen. A fixed-length leash between four and six feet allows enough room for comfortable exploration during a walk, but still keeps the reactive dog close by you.

High-value rewards are critical when working on changing the hearts and minds of reactive dogs. The moist, meaty treat that you use should "trump" the target across the road, meaning your dog will be able to focus on it and you instead of the other dog or person. I like to use treats like hot dogs, pieces of chicken, cheese, or lunch meats like turkey slices—basically, items so savory that you're tempted to eat them yourself! It also helps to have easily accessible pockets or a treat pouch so that you can get to the treats without a struggle. You'll be rewarding your dog frequently, so you should be able to grab the treats without fumbling.

I've worked with people who have tried using treats in the past only to discover that their dog won't eat them. This could be a case of either using the wrong type of treat—something dull that doesn't trump the environmental distractions—or more likely it's a case of trying to feed the dog when he's already deeply enmeshed in a reactive response. When a dog has tipped over into fight-or-flight response, it's nearly impossible to regain his focus. Eating is no longer possible when faced with what seems like a life-or-death scenario unfolding before the dog. Even though you might not have had success with treats in the past, used properly they *will* help your dog to feel more comfortable around targets.

Some dogs benefit from switching from a collar to a no-pull body harness as described on page 104. These types of harnesses are designed to gently inhibit pulling using straps around the front of the dog's body.

Clicker 101

Clicker training is a joyful and creative way to work with dogs. It's my method of choice, and it has helped me reach many a reactive dog. If your dog has never been clicker trained, it's imperative that you help him understand what the clicker means before you start working on the important stuff outside. To begin, grab your dog, the clicker, and a handful of treats. When your dog is close to you, place the clicker near your waist and click it once (it's not a computer mouse, so no double-clicking is required). Immediately give him a high-value treat. He doesn't have to do anything fancy initially, just make sure he keeps all four paws on the floor and doesn't jump up as you work. Remember to keep the clicker up near your waist—it's not a remote control, so you don't have to point it at your dog to make it work! Move around the room and click and treat your dog just for remaining close to you. Then ask your dog to sit, and click exactly when his rump hits the ground. (The clicker is a way of saying, "That's it! I like what you just did!") Immediately follow up with the food reward. Repeat the process, asking your dog for sits or downs, and click and treat when he performs the behavior. Repeat the process over the course of a few days. You want your dog to have a good grasp of what the clicker means before you begin working with it while on leash.

Taking some of the tension off your dog's neck can similarly diffuse some of the tension of the encounter.

Finally, consider using a clicker. As discussed in the sections on crate training and leash pulling, a clicker is a plastic matchbook-sized device that's used to mark behavior. It serves as a "bridge" between the desired behavior—which in this scenario will initially be anything other than reactive behavior—and the food reward. It's a very precise way of saying, "That's it—I like what you just did!" The clicker is particularly powerful when working on reactive behavior because it cuts through any environmental clutter and allows the dog to understand *exactly* what he did right. The clicker allows you to mark even the smallest steps towards improvement, which helps to keep a potentially frustrating training experience positive for both parties.

If you opt to skip the clicker, use a clear short marker word that marks the moment when your dog acted appropriately. As mentioned previously, I like to use the word "yup" because it's not a word that's muddied from frequent conversational use (like "yes"), and the *p* at the end has a definitive sound. You can "charge up" the word in the same way that you do with the clicker.

Getting Started

Working on leash reactivity is a fairly straightforward process, but the reality of putting it into practice isn't always easy. It requires that you're focused and ready to train every time you step outside with your dog. It requires that you're observant about everything happening around you, and everything your dog is saying with his body. And it requires that you stay upbeat no matter how challenging the process gets. The beginning stages of working on leash reactivity are much like learning a new dance: you'll feel awkward and uncomfortable at first, and you might step on feet (or paws!). Gradually the "dance" will become more natural for you, and eventually, with practice, your canine partner will fall in seamless step with you.

The principle behind the training is to change how your dog perceives and feels about his former targets. Instead of using punishment to suppress his reactions to the targets, as Annie's trainer tried to do with Jax, you will use food to help your dog change the way he feels when faced with people or other dogs. If your timing is good (and with practice it will be!), your dog might even *welcome* seeing a strange dog on the street!

Initially, your dog will learn that when he sees something that upsets him he gets "paid" with something delicious. Your goal is to help him make an association between the bad thing and something very good. Once your dog begins to make the association between the target and the food rewards, you'll require that he perform simple behaviors in order to *earn* his food reward.

If possible, use a trustworthy friend with a mellow dog as targets during choreographed training sessions, where you can direct their movements as you work through the exercises. Unfortunately, this isn't always an option, so equipping yourself to work in the unpredictable great outdoors is a must. The reality is that the process is straightforward on paper, but much more unpredictable in the real world. Because of that, setbacks are inevitable but not uncommon.

One of the most important first steps of this type of training is determining your dog's *threshold,* or the point at which he tips over from being okay about seeing a target to reacting to it. Once your dog is snarling and barking at the target, it's too late to try to change his response, so the goal is to catch your dog when he *notices* the target but hasn't committed to reacting to it. This threshold distance varies from dog to dog. For some, a dog on the distant horizon is enough to elicit a reaction; for others, the dog can be just a half block away before the barking begins. The size of and reactions from the other dog can factor in as well. Your dog might be okay with a quiet medium-size dog at closer range than he is with a larger vocal dog three blocks away. Pay attention to your dog and watch for that moment when he locks on to the target but hasn't begun reacting, noting the distance between him and the target. Maintain this distance as you work through the

During training it's critical that you maintain a buffer between your dog and the "target" that causes a reaction.

following exercises—you don't want to breach it if at all possible. (Unfortunately, you can't always predict what's coming around the corner, so accidents will happen.)

Watch your dog for obvious indicators of increasing stress when he spots the target, like a hard stare, orienting his body toward the target, yawning, stiffness, raised hackles, or panting (either a sudden occurrence of panting or a closed-mouth cessation of panting, depending on the temperature and your dog's activity level). Once your dog is exhibiting these types of signals, you're close to "losing" him to the target, at which point he might tip over into reactivity. Increase your buffer zone if necessary to keep your dog comfortable and able to work with you.

Begin your walk with your treats and dog on your left side, and your leash and clicker in your right hand. (You can reverse hands if you're a leftie.) Keeping these tools in separate hands will prevent you from fumbling when it comes time to deliver treats. Your dog should be on your left

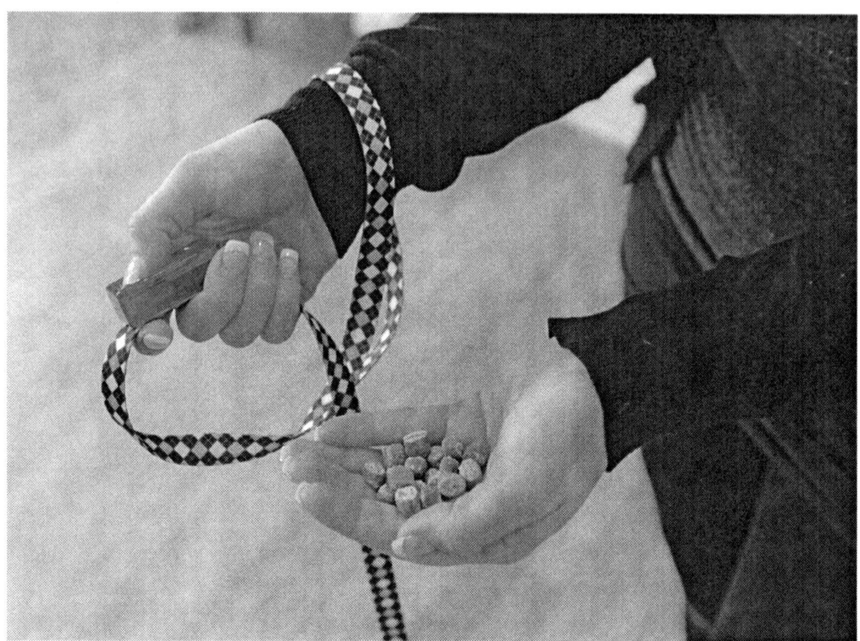

Dedicate one hand for the clicker and leash and the other hand for treat dispensing.

side near the hand that will be delivering treats, and the leash will drape across the front of your knees.

Begin click-treating your dog the moment he spots a target. Make sure that he actually sees it—although click treats are always appreciated, they won't have the desired impact unless your dog starts to make the association between the target on the horizon and the sudden appearance of delicious food. *Continue* click-treating as long as the other dog is in sight, maintaining your predetermined buffer from the other dog. Do your best to remain upbeat and cheerful as you reward your dog, praising happily as you work through the exercise. Ideally, you're clicking for the absence of an aggressive reaction, and if you've read your dog properly, the buffer will keep your dog from tipping over into reactivity. If you find that your dog is taking treats from your hand but keeping his eyes fixed on the target and getting increasingly agitated, you can "change the temperature" of the scenario by clicking and tossing the treats on the ground in front of your dog. Encouraging your dog to pick up treats on the ground is an easy way to hit the "reset button" and prevent him from fixating on a target.

The concept of nonstop click-treating while the target is in view might be a difficult one to accept, particularly because your dog might not seem to be doing anything worthy of rewarding, but it's critical that the flow of treats continues as long as the target is around. This process is your first step in helping your dog to understand that the target equals very good things: when another dog appears, it rains treats. You can stop the steady flow of treats when the target disappears.

Although you can't control what's coming around the corner, try to keep your dog from getting to a point where he feels that he has no choice but to react. Cross the road, duck behind parked cars, walk up driveways, and do whatever you can to keep that safety buffer between you and the target so that your dog doesn't tip over into reactivity. I like to use a teach-as-you-go cue to encourage a dog to follow along with me when I need to make a sudden direction change. I say, "This way!" in a cheerful voice and praise the dog for coming with me. It's another easy "reset" behavior that can help to diffuse an escalating moment.

What happens if someone sneaks up and you're caught off guard? *Don't stop doing what you've been doing!* Say, for example, a dog rounds the corner and you're nearly face-to-face. Your dog is barking like crazy and it feels like all progress is lost. What now? Although it seems counterintuitive to continue feeding your dog while he's reacting to a target, remind yourself that the food is helping to change your dog's underlying emotional state. The knee-jerk reaction many people have to this directive is, "But I'm rewarding my dog for bad behavior! Won't this encourage his reactivity?" It won't. The positive association with the food is so strong that it outweighs any accidental reinforcement of the barking. It feels wrong, but it's not, I promise! The work you're doing during the rest of the walk, when you maintain the buffer and keep your dog calm, is chipping away at that reactivity one click at a time.

Advocating to Keep the Peace

Being your dog's advocate is particularly important when dealing with leash issues. Well-intentioned strangers might try to bring their dog too close to yours (even though he's at the end of his leash snarling), or attempt to pet your fearful reactive dog. Be forthright when people try to approach you and your dog. Move away as you tell them, "Please stay away, my dog doesn't handle other dogs/people/bikes well, and we're in training for it." Walk in the opposite direction if necessary (telling your dog, "This way!"); just don't let anyone force you into an interaction that you know won't end well. There's a new movement that recommends using a yellow ribbon on a dog's leash to signify the need for space. The concept isn't universally known yet, but it can't hurt to add a yellow ribbon to your reactive dog's leash!

You should continue with this first step of the training process—raining treats on your dog when a target appears beyond the buffer zone—until you begin to see a spark of realization in your dog when the target appears on the scene. How will you know when that's happened? In most cases it's as simple as a glance away from the target and in your direction, as if to say, "Hey, there's a dog over there. That means I get a goody, right?" This is a major victory! It means that your dog has begun to make the positive association to the target required to bring about change. How long does it usually take before a dog offers this type of response? It depends on the dog, the intensity of his reactions in the past (were they just blustery barks or did your dog seem like he was ready for a throw-down?), how long the reactivity has been happening (is it a newer issue or have you been dealing with it for years?), and how diligent *you* are with the training process. I've seen a dog have this "aha!" moment within the first lesson, and I've worked with others that took weeks before they made the association.

From this point you can begin to make your dog work a little in order to earn his treats when you see a target at the edge of his buffer zone. Instead of giving a nonstop stream of treats when a target appears, wait for your dog to glance at you —thereby showing an understanding that target equals treat—and then click-treat. Continue walking and look for that glance at you again, but this time praise him and make him hold your gaze for slightly longer before you click-treat. Or, if your dog has trouble looking at you for longer than a split-second during a walk, you could time the click to when he looks *away* from the dog instead of waiting for him to look at you. The difference with this new step is that you're clicking your dog for *consciously doing* something when he sees the target instead of just click-treating to make the association between the target and treat.

Once your dog is predictably offering you behaviors that show he understands the connection between target and treat, like looking away from the other dog or looking at you, you can begin to reduce the buffer zone you've been using. Again, there is no concrete time frame for making this change; your dog's behavior will dictate when you can begin. Changing the intensity of the target ("It's closer! It's scarier!") might require that you go back to the rapid-fire click-treating until you see your dog once again acknowledging the target's presence in a positive fashion, but your dog's happy history with this process should make the learning curve quicker this time. Work on decreasing the distance from the target gradually, always watching your dog to make sure that he's comfortable with the changes you're making. As before, watch for your dog offering acknowledgment behaviors like pointedly looking away from the target or, even better, looking at you. Continue to gradually decrease your distance from targets, always letting your dog set the pace for how quickly that happens. As your

Surprise Backslide

You and your dog have been doing great and then suddenly—*boom!*—it's as if you've never had a single lesson. These unpredictable backslides can be disheartening. However, they're an understandable part of the process because our dogs are thinking beings that operate under the influence of their feelings and surroundings. They're not computers waiting to be programmed! Maybe your dog has been cooped up for too long and hasn't had enough exercise, and the barking dog on the horizon is just too much to resist. Or perhaps the treats you've been using for the past three weeks have lost their allure. It's natural to have setbacks during the training process, but it's important to consider the reasons for them before heaping the blame on your dog, or becoming disenchanted with the process.

dog's behavior improves you can begin to transition off the clicker to a verbal marker like "yup!" The clicker's precision and clarity are helpful during the formative stages of the training process, but aren't necessary as your dog begins to understand the process.

The Road to Recovery

How do you know when you're "done" training this behavior? Once again, it depends on your dog. I suggest keeping a supply of treats in your pocket even after your dog has demonstrated that he's able to accept targets of all varieties at all intensities. Offering your dog a surprise treat for gracefully coping with a target helps to keep the new and improved behavior alive. We tend to want to rush to get rid of treats, as if using them somehow diminishes the power of the relationship we have with our dogs. (I regularly hear the refrain, "But I want my dog to work for me, not for the food!") Though your bond with your dog is an incredible motivator, during the training process you must bow to the power of a primary reinforcer, something that is inherently rewarding like food. Offering your dog a food reward for passing by a target without comment—even after he's been doing it for a while—reminds him that he's got the right idea. You don't have to give him a treat every time, as you did during the beginning stages of the process, but these occasional rewards will keep those positive responses coming.

eleven

ATTENTION-SEEKING BEHAVIOR

It's not always easy to recognize attention-seeking behavior for what it truly is when it's first taking root. The barking, pawing, nose bumps, jumping up, or pacing might just seem like typical nuisance behaviors that aren't a big deal. The real problems begin when your dog learns that these types of behaviors actually *work* for him, meaning he understands that nudging your hand nonstop will eventually make you pet him, or bouncing off the door repeatedly will make you open it for him. These accidental reinforcements of nuisance behaviors—giving in to your dog and giving him what he wants even though you don't like the way he asked for it—set the stage for cementing them. Dogs do what works for them, and if barking or pawing or jumping up gives him access to a desired resource, the dog will continue performing the behavior.

Case Study: Simone loved her French Bulldog, Walker, but he had a few behaviors that made life with him difficult. Simone worked from home and often spent time on conference calls with clients, during which Walker barked incessantly if she wasn't paying attention to him. She did her best to pet him and toss his ball during the calls, but she couldn't always interact with him when she had to take notes or work on her computer. The moment she looked away from him he stood right beside her and barked his raspy unmistakable bark until she stopped what she was doing and leaned down to interact with him. Her clients often remarked about the noise, which embarrassed her. She was stressed every time she had to make a call, whether it was for business or just a check-in with her parents. Walker could hear Simone picking up the phone from anywhere in her condo, so even when she tried to place calls when he was sound asleep, he'd come running the moment he heard it rattle on the table. It seemed like a game to him—the only time he barked and pestered her was when she was on the phone.

Possible Outcome One: Walker's barking escalates to the point where Simone can barely hear the person on the other end of the call. She resorts to locking him in her bedroom, only to have him bark louder and longer during the imprisonment. She can still hear him though the walls of her small condo, though the sound is somewhat muffled and he can no longer jump on her and nip during the calls. Unfortunately, Simone's neighbors can also hear Walker's commotion, and it doesn't take long before the angry notes start appearing on her front door. She realizes that things have gotten out of control when an official letter from her condo association shows up, informing her that additional nuisance complaints from her neighbors will result in a $100.00 fine per violation.

Possible Outcome Two: Simone's boss pulls her aside after an on-site meeting and tells her that she needs to start working from the office two days a week. He doesn't specify why, but Simone is sure that it's because her clients have commented about Walker's barking during calls. The change in schedule doesn't sit well with Walker, who barks and howls nearly the entire time Simone is out of the house. Simone feels guilty because she has less time to interact with her dog. She knows that she's not coming close to burning through his young dog energy, and while she would love to send him to doggie day care while she's at the office, she just can't afford it. Simone feels a combination of frustration with her dog for "making" her have to report to the office, and anger at herself for allowing Walker to get so out of control.

What Is Attention-Seeking Behavior?

Attention-seeking behavior is any disruptive strategy that a dog employs to gain access to a desired resource, whether it's dinner, an open door, or your attention. The behaviors can range from silly to life altering, like Walker's barking. Attention-seeking behaviors aren't always awful; my Boston Terrier Zeke learned that I would stop anything I was doing whenever he rolled onto his back and exposed his belly. If I was focused on something else, like my computer, he'd huff and puff quietly while in position until I looked over and saw him posed like a beached seal. It was an adorable attention-seeking behavior that I loved, so I was always happy to interrupt my work to pet his fat stomach. That said, most typical attention-seeking behaviors aren't as appreciated. They include:

- **Barking or whining:** The dog's barking isn't at something he hears or sees (alarm barking like this is covered in Chapter 13) but rather is usually directed toward a person in the household who isn't paying attention to the dog. He may also bark or whine to get access to something, like dinner.
- **Pawing or nose-bumping:** Depending on the dog's size, pawing can be a painful communication strategy. Many dogs employ this

technique to encourage petting, but I've worked with many dogs who have pawed or nose-bumped to get more treats. (I call it "mugging.")

- **Jumping up:** This behavior can range from jumping up on people for attention (jumpy greetings, which are slightly different, are covered in Chapter 5), or jumping up on furniture and counters to get you to tune in to them. Any attention, even angry attention when you tell the dog to get off, "works" for the dog.
- **Pushing toys at you:** Dropping toys in your lap or at your feet to engage you in play is one of the less egregious attention-seeking behaviors, but it can become disruptive if you're trying get something done or if you have guests in the house.
- **Playing keep away:** Some dogs learn that when they grab household items, you'll chase. It's not that the dog necessarily wants the item in question; the dog wants the *fun* that comes from your undivided attention as you run after him.
- **Grooming behaviors:** When a dog scratches or licks at himself for an extended period of time, it's normal to see if something is wrong. Is he scratching because he has an allergy, or fleas? Is he licking at a hot spot? Attention-seeking dogs pick up on the concern we exhibit when we check on them for excessive grooming, thereby cementing the behavior as a viable way to gain our focus. It took my Olive only a few rounds of excessive early morning scratching to realize that it would make me get out of bed to check on her.

Because these behaviors work for the dog, they stay in the repertoire. Getting rid of them can be a challenge because of their strong reinforcement history. Many of us find the attention-seeking behavior so annoying that we give in to what the dog wants just to make it stop, not realizing that each time we do so the dog learns that the behavior is a practical strategy. Although throwing the ball for your dog when he's whining might make it possible for you to hear the dialogue on TV, you've just set the stage for the behavior to continue. Your dog learned, "If I whine loudly near my person when he's sitting in that chair, *eventually* he will throw the ball for me!"

Some dogs are chronically understimulated, and resorting to attention-seeking behaviors is the only way they know how to get their people to interact with them. They learn that when they're quiet they're ignored, but when they're spinning in circles and barking, their people might actually look at them and talk to them. To the attention-starved dog, even yelling counts as an act of community. We might feel that we're punishing the dog for the behavior, but the dog brain reads it as much-desired acknowledgment

("My person sees me!"), so the behavior remains. The same goes for dogs that are underexercised. Dogs will find their own fun if adequate entertainment isn't provided, which can manifest in attention-seeking behaviors like grabbing shoes and playing keep away.

Mindfulness and Attention-Seeking Behavior

Attention-seeking behavior starts innocently enough. In Simone and Walker's case it was a series of playful barks during a day when Simone was on several conference calls. Simone shushed him and played tug to keep him quiet every time he made a noise, and thus a habit was quickly born. Every time Simone picked up the phone and focused on something other than Walker, he made it his business to regain her focus by barking at her, and every time he barked, Simone paid attention to him. Walker very quickly learned that barking *worked.*

Mindful interactions are particularly important when dealing with burgeoning attention-seeking behaviors. Reminding yourself of the important questions, *"Do I like this behavior? Do I want it to continue?"* will help you determine how to respond to the behavior. If you prefer that your dog refrain from barking at you when he wants his dinner, simply don't feed him his dinner while he's barking at you. Don't let the barking work for him. If you don't want your dog to whine and place his toy in your lap while you're watching TV, don't engage him in a game of fetch when he's being pushy and noisy. Keep in mind that in some scenarios you can unintentionally reinforce the attention-seeking behavior by just *looking* at your dog.

If you take a step back and consider the behavior your dog is offering you, then you can make a better decision about how to respond (or not respond) to your dog's demands. If you don't like your dog's behavior, why would you give him what he wants? It's a simple process to undertake before an attention-seeking behavior becomes rooted. Once the behavior is well established, however, it takes time and attention to untrain it. Let's get started to do just that.

A Tired Dog Is a Content Dog

Many dogs that engage in extreme attention-seeking behavior share a common problem: they're underexercised both in body and mind. Exercising your dog more won't necessarily cure his pushy ball playing or whining for dinner, but it will reduce some of his demanding behavior. Consider the

Taking the time to exercise and wear out your dog can dramatically decrease attention-seeking behaviors.

motivation behind the attention-seeking behavior beyond just getting your focus; if your dog keeps going into the laundry basket and parading in front of you with your dirty socks in the hopes that you'll chase after him, he's a prime candidate for increased exercise.

To resolve the exercise problem, first know that a walk around the block doesn't cut it. Most dogs need daily pant-inducing activities to put a dent in their energy reserves, and if they don't get that type of exercise they can resort to the frustrating behaviors detailed on pages 156–157. Scheduling predictable activity dates with your dog is an easy way to work through some of his pent-up energy and bonds you both in the process. Making a commitment to focus your attention on your dog at *least* once a day (in addition to regularly scheduled walks) should be a no-brainer, but because we're all so busy, our dogs often miss out. I've trained both my dogs and myself well: they know that when I get home from work we either go out in the yard for a play session or in our basement if the weather is bad. The time I invest playing with them ensures that I'll be able to focus on my "homework" without feeling guilty and having to endure their sad faces staring at me.

The following games are some of my favorites:

When playing fetch ask your dog to sit before throwing the toy.

- **Tug:** Tug is a great game to burn off energy because it doesn't require much space, dogs of all ages can play it, and you can incorporate basic training into the game to turn it into a lesson. Playing tug with rules can help keep the game civilized, so check out the game overview in Chapter 3.
- **Fetch:** Most of us go on autopilot when we play fetch with our dogs, but actually engaging in the game with your dog turns it from rote to exciting. Teach your dog to drop the ball when asked, use multiple toys to speed up the retrieval rate, and throw the ball in unpredictable directions and distances to keep the game fresh.
- **Hide-and-seek:** This is a great rainy-day game when you can't get outside and play with your dog. Put your dog in a "stay" or have a helper hold him lightly around the shoulders. Leave the room and then hide in a closet or behind the shower curtain and tell your dog, "Come find me!" You can give your dog hints by making noises, but try not to give too many clues so that your dog learns to tap into his scenting abilities in order to discover your hiding spot.
- **Hide the toy:** Teach your dog to hunt for a hidden toy as described on page 53, or use a treat or bone if your dog isn't toy motivated. Get creative with your hiding spots as your dog gets better at finding the

hidden objects. Scenting games that engage a dog's brain (and nose!) do wonders to tire dogs out.

- **Trick training:** Spend a few minutes teaching your dog something new and fun, like "sit pretty" or "take a bow" using the clicker. Because trick training really makes a dog think, it does wonders to take the edge off a busy dog.

Occupied and Happy

Simone could have avoided the stress caused by Walker's attention-seeking barking if she had opted to give him something to do instead of giving in to him. There's a huge variety of treat-dispensing toys on the market that cater to every canine play preference, from toys that encourage the dog to be active in order to dislodge the treats to those that require the dog to sit down for a concentrated and prolonged chew session. Because Simone knew that Walker harassed her when she was on the phone (remember, predictable problems are preventable), she could have given him a treat toy prior to getting on the phone. Because giving him the treat toy effectively

Giving your dog a treat-stuffed busy toy is an excellent way to keep him content, happy, and out of trouble.

interrupted his barky behavioral chain, over time she could have tapered off giving him the toys until he was able to rest quietly without one while she was on the phone.

The dog that whines and pesters when it's time to unwind in the evening could also benefit from a busy toy or a bone. Giving your dog something to do any time you know that you can't focus on your dog (and when you know that he'll likely *demand* your focus despite what you're doing) is a simple way to manage the problem. I liken it to a babysitter for your dog—it's a way to ensure that your dog is content while you attend to other matters. Variety is important, though. Your dog might be fascinated with a bone or toy initially but decide that it's old news after a few days. Make sure that you have several options to keep your dog engaged, and switch them out frequently. Everything old is new again when you reintroduce a toy that's been kept in the closet for a few weeks!

While plush stuffed toys are great fun for shared play with your dog, they're not a wise choice when you want to keep your dog constructively occupied. Plush toys aren't constructed to stand up to prolonged (and sometimes frustrated) attention, and most dogs become surgeons in an attempt to rip out the squeaker. Instead, look for well-constructed hard rubber busy toys that have crevices to fill with treats to challenge the canine brain. Again, offering your dog a treat toy isn't the guaranteed solution for every attention-seeking behavior, but it's a huge help for many of them.

Attention-Seeking Behaviors—The Obvious Secret

It's clear that dogs engage in attention-seeking behaviors because they work for them. So what's the easiest way to short-circuit the pattern? Don't let the behaviors work! The goal is to *ignore* the behavior that you want to get rid of and *acknowledge* the behavior that you'd like to see replace it. My experiences with Olive have given me many opportunities to put this advice into practice on a daily basis, particularly when she was an adolescent. She attempted to employ nearly every technique listed on pages 156–157 in order to either get me to pay attention to her or get desired resources like bones, toys, or dinner. Because I knew how annoying the behaviors could become over time (mindful interactions to the rescue!), I never let her attention-seeking strategies get her what she wanted. That said, she was a determined dog, so it was a bumpy few weeks as she figured out which behaviors worked to get what she wanted instead of the brute-force behaviors that she assumed would work.

For example, if your dog whines and fusses at you when it's his dinnertime, walk away from him and ignore him the moment he opens his mouth. Don't go anywhere near the food-prep area until he's quiet. (Initially he might only be able to refrain from making noise for a moment.) Praise him while he's quiet and begin dishing out his food. If he starts again, put the bowl down and walk away. Basically, your dog *attracts* you to the food-prep area when he's quiet, and he *repels* you from it when he's noisy. You might have to quit and resume a few times until he understands that whining makes you stop and being quiet makes you continue. Serve him his meal only after he has remained quiet during preparation.

The second part of the process—acknowledging the behaviors you like—is critical. You not only want to squelch the inappropriate behaviors, but you also want to help your dog understand which behaviors will get you to interact with him. Acknowledge your dog any time he's resting quietly or doing something that you appreciate, like playing with a toy or chewing a bone. It feels counterintuitive to interrupt a dog that's being quiet and "good," but it's a simple way of helping your dog understand what types of behaviors truly work to get your focus. The pushy dog gets ignored. The polite dog gets acknowledged.

Olive used to bark at me in the morning when she wanted attention. I ignored the barking (which wasn't easy because it's very shrill) and waited until she was resting quietly before I acknowledged her. Sometimes it took a good ten minutes of on-and-off barking before she realized that her strategy wasn't working, and she'd give up. I made a point to praise her and pet her for being quiet, and then invited her to play tug with me. I wanted her to know that barking got her nothing, but calm got her everything. In time she figured out that her constant pacing and commentary were just barking in the wind, and she abandoned the strategy. Now our mornings are peaceful, and she receives more petting and kisses from me than she wants because I wind up waking her from her post-breakfast naps!

Before It Gets Better . . .

You might have already heard that ignoring unwanted behavior is the best way to make it go away. Perhaps you even tried it for a little while, only to discover that it *wasn't* working, and your dog was pawing/whining/barking more than ever. What gives?

If you've attempted to ignore the unwanted behavior and then determined that you just couldn't deal with it for a second longer and gave in, you actually made the behavior even *more* resistant to extinction! Giving in when your dog is at his most crazed after ignoring the behavior for a while teaches him that he not only has to keep at it but also that his most dramatic displays are the ones that finally crack the code.

Part of the challenge of ignoring a cemented attention-seeking behavior is that dogs go through what's called an "extinction burst" just prior to giving up on it. It's similar to what happens when an impatient person is waiting for an elevator; the person hits the button to summon the elevator and if it doesn't come immediately, the person hits the button again and again until they give up and wait quietly. Your dog might demonstrate his extinction burst by performing the attention-seeking behavior louder, longer, or more often before it finally disappears. Remember that your dog's dramatic last-ditch effort to make the attention-seeking behavior work means that you're almost there. Don't quit!

What If It Comes Back?

There's a chance that even after all of your hard work ignoring the attention-seeking behavior and reinforcing the preferred behavior that the undesired behavior might spontaneously reappear. Perhaps your dog has learned that you'll no longer pet him when he bumps his nose into your leg, but the first time you have company over he's at it again, bumping you *and* your guest. This is yet another normal but challenging part of the extinction process. Just because the behavior has been squelched doesn't mean that it's been completely unlearned. It's still there, buried in his dog brain, and there's a chance that it might spontaneously erupt. But if you stick to the program and make sure that your dog doesn't get rewarded, once again the attention-seeking behavior will go away.

twelve

PICKY EATERS

It's a foregone conclusion that most dogs love to eat anything and everything, from cardboard to mulch, rocks, roadkill, and even fecal matter. There's a reason behind the word "chowhound"! Some dogs, however, are so selective about what they eat that their people go to great lengths to make sure that they consume something, *anything,* at mealtimes. Some selective diners are born, some are made, and many are a combination of the two. That said, it's possible to help your picky eater learn to eat with enjoyment, if not gusto.

Case Study: Phyllis doted over her Cavalier King Charles Spaniel Sam. He had an overflowing toy basket, several plush beds, a wardrobe of clothing, and handmade porcelain bowls with little crowns on them. Phyllis made sure that Sam had the best of everything, including his dog food. When it came time to transition to adult food, she selected a brand that had

Picky eaters can make mealtimes challenging.

Cause for Concern

If your normally hungry dog suddenly turns his nose up at his food, he might be suffering from a health issue. Problems like intestinal issues, parasites, or pain within the mouth like broken teeth, swollen gums, or objects trapped between teeth can cause a dog to stop eating. Contact your veterinarian if your dog's eating patterns change suddenly.

photos of fruits and vegetables on the bag, convinced that it was the healthiest option for her best friend.

Sam had never been a big eater as a puppy. Phyllis often coaxed him to eat his food, kneeling by him as he picked at the kibble in the bowl. Sometimes she added cheese or bacon to his food, which resulted in him eating the embellishments but not the actual dog food. When she switched to his adult food he became even pickier, skipping meals if she didn't put extra goodies in it. Phyllis supplemented Sam's diet with a variety of dog treats from the grocery store, and often shared her dinner with him if he hadn't cleaned out his bowl.

Possible Outcome One: Sam continues off-and-on hunger strikes, so Phyllis compensates by sharing all of her meals with him. She doles out a portion of his kibble every day but it remains untouched in the bowl. His appetite is actually robust—he's game to eat anything that Phyllis eats, from scrambled eggs loaded with butter to fatty pieces of steak, but he won't touch his dog food. One morning after a hearty breakfast of bacon Phyllis notices that Sam seems mellow and disconnected, as if he's not feeling well. He walks with his back hunched, and after he vomits Phyllis decides that the symptoms are worthy of a trip to the vet. Sam is diagnosed with acute pancreatitis, an inflammation and swelling of the pancreas partially due to his high-fat diet. Sam is kept at the vet office for twenty-four hours and given fluids and pain medication to help manage his symptoms. Phyllis is filled with guilt for contributing to his discomfort.

Possible Outcome Two: Because Sam doesn't seem to enjoy dog food, Phyllis buys a different bag every time she goes to the grocery store, hoping that she'll stumble on a type that he'll eat. She continues to supplement his meals with treats and bits of her dinner. The constantly changing diet doesn't seem to help Sam at all. His coat is dull and thin. He always has an odor, even after a bath. His stools are loose and difficult to pick up. Sam's picky eating is a constant challenge for Phyllis, and the difficulty of finding a food that helps him to thrive is evident in his unhealthy appearance.

Are picky eaters born or made? Sam was probably a selective eater to begin with, and Phyllis accidentally nurtured his habit with disastrous results. Picky eating might not seem like a big deal, but ensuring that your dog is eating a nutritious diet is critical for long-term health. What could Phyllis have done to prevent Sam's selective eating and dependence on people food?

A Few Thoughts about Dog Food

People often come into my store and ask me for "the best" dog food, but there is no one food that's a perfect fit for every dog. Finding the right food for your dog means finding one that agrees with his system and is healthful, which depends on factors like the dog's age, weight, energy and activity levels, environmental factors, and, of course, his preferences. While this isn't going to be an in-depth look at dog-food nutrition, I do want to point out a few things to consider when selecting your dog's food.

- Look for a food that has an identifiable protein as the first ingredient. Food labels list the concentration of ingredients in descending order, so the first few items on the label are the most important. Select a food with the first ingredient that's a named meat, like chicken, beef, or lamb. Don't be concerned if you see the meat listed as "chicken meal"—meal is the protein with the water removed. Avoid foods that list ambiguous proteins like just "meat" or "animal byproduct," which can include things like feet, bones, blood, and organs.
- Watch out for foods that list fillers near the top of the ingredient list, like "ground yellow corn," "corn gluten meal," "wheat flour." While it's impossible to create a kibble without *any* fillers, foods with heavy concentrations of fillers might contribute to weight gain or allergic reactions. Plus they're just not healthy.
- Avoid dog food with different-colored kibble. Adding coloring (basically, unnecessary chemicals) to dog food does nothing for the dog—the "red 40" and "yellow 6" are there to make the food look more interesting to *you.*
- Finally, avoid foods that contain sweeteners. Dogs don't need sugar in their food, but many manufacturers use it to literally sweeten the pot if the food isn't palatable on its own. Sometimes the sweetener is camouflaged—it might not jump out at you when it's called sucrose or corn syrup, but it's still an unhealthy sweetener.

While finding a nutritious food is an important first step in ensuring your dog's optimum health, it's not necessarily the silver-bullet solution for a picky eater. You might find that your dog is even less inclined to dive in to a healthy new food if he's been picking at a sugar-filled "kid's cereal" type

Taste Test

Rather than investing in bag after bag of food only to have your dog turn his nose up at each one, ask your retailer for a few sample sizes of healthy dog foods and let your dog choose for himself. Place each type of food on small plates and opt for the food that your dog happily eats.

of dog food, or if you've been supplementing his diet with treats or people food. The following tips will help your dog break the picky habit and set him on the road to healthier eating.

On People Food and Treats

Dogs that are "born finicky" do exist. Smaller breeds like Yorkshire Terriers and Pomeranians seem more likely to turn their noses up at their dog food. That said, some dogs are accidentally encouraged to be more selective about what they eat because their regular diet is supplemented by treats and people food throughout the day, much like what happened with Phyllis and Sam.

Dog treats definitely have a place in a dog's life, but they're not meant to be meal replacements. Healthy, natural, USA-made dog treats are a great way to reward your dog for a job well done. Because training is a lifetime endeavor with your dog, it makes sense to continue to offer your dog a small treat when he responds to a request. (My dogs still get a fingernail-sized goody when they come when I call or after a nail trim.) Giving treats "just because" isn't a good idea from a training perspective or a healthy eating perspective, particularly when you're dealing with a picky eater. Dogs that are constantly fed treats are clever enough to realize that if they "hold out" they'll eventually get something else to eat. (Plus they'll learn that they don't have to work in order to earn a treat!)

The same goes for giving your dog too much of your food. While there are some great recipes for home-cooked meals for dogs (and some delicious add-ins discussed in the next section), giving your dog the food from your plate—the seasoned creamy salty stuff you eat—isn't healthy and can encourage picky eating. While some of the foods that we eat are also healthy for dogs, feeding fatty, highly seasoned people food to a finicky dog can encourage the dog's selective eating.

While occasional plate cleanings are fine, allowing your dog to eat too much rich, seasoned human food is unhealthy.

Add-ins for the Win

Sometimes all it takes to kick-start a reticent eater is a little bit of something extra (and appropriate) in the bowl along with his high-quality dog food. The mixers should be an enticement to eat but not the sole consumable of the meal. Any add-ins should constitute less than 15 percent of your dog's nutritionally balanced food, and can be weaned over time. That said, adding fresh, healthy foods to your dog's food is a fine way to improve his store-bought dog food. It would be awfully boring for us to eat the exact same food every day, so why should we make our dogs do it?

Any one of the following might be enough to convince your dog to eat with gusto:

- **Low-salt chicken broth:** Add diluted broth to your dog's food and let it sit for a few minutes before you serve it. This changes the consistency of the kibble.
- **Plain low-fat yogurt:** Yogurt's beneficial bacteria is good for dogs with digestive issues, plus most dogs find the creamy consistency very palatable.

Made by You

Opting to home cook your dog's meals instead of feeding traditional kibble can be a wonderful and healthy way to encourage a finicky eater to dig in, particularly if the dog has ongoing digestive upsets, or eats a commercial dog food for a few days but then stops. Feeding a home-prepared diet can change the way a picky dog views meal-times, but it requires a plan and careful research. Dogs must be fed a complete and balanced diet in order to maintain maximum health, so finding a home-prepared meal plan that takes this need into account is critical. Many fussy eaters thrive when they're fed a balanced home-made diet. Making a home-prepared diet every day is labor intensive, but the results can be nothing short of amazing. For more information on cooking meals for your dog, check out *K9 Kitchen - Your Dogs' Diet: The Truth Behind the Hype* by Monica Segal and also *Dr. Becker's Real Food for Healthy Dogs and Cats* by Beth Taylor.

- **Fruits and vegetables:** Mashed bananas, berries like blueberries, apples chopped into small pieces and cooked, and chopped carrots are healthy upgrades that can encourage eating. Keep in mind that the size and consistency of the fruit or veggie can have an impact on whether the dog will eat it. (A picky dog might not enjoy whole uncooked baby carrots mixed in with his crunchy food.)
- **Coconut oil:** Coconut oil is considered a miracle in a jar because it helps to support overall canine health. Most dogs find the taste irresistible, and the benefits of adding it to your dog's diet are numerous. From improving digestion, to helping itchy dogs find relief, to reducing the risk of certain cancers, this add-in can do much more than just encourage your dog to eat his food. Coconut oil should be gradually added to a dog's food over the course of a week, ending up at one teaspoon per ten pounds of body weight, or one tablespoon per thirty pounds.
- **High-quality canned dog food:** Look for canned foods with named meats near the beginning of the ingredients list and limited byproducts.

The Feeding Station

Sometimes seemingly picky eating isn't just about the food itself. Surprisingly, even the *bowl* can have a bearing on how willingly a dog eats. Sliding bowls, noisy bowls, and even the shape and depth of the bowl can all make a sensitive dog less likely to eat. I once worked with a dog whose people noticed that she suddenly seemed less interested in meals. (They had already visited the vet and gotten a clean bill of health.) After Q&A I discovered that they were using a stainless steel bowl and the new dog tag she was wearing kept hitting the side of it as she tried to eat. The loud clanging distressed her, so she would only pick at a few bites before giving up on the meal. Her people switched to a recycled bamboo bowl and the finicky eating disappeared. Similarly, bowls that "walk" as the dog digs in can cause problems. Millie used to stop eating before she reached the bottom of the bowl because the stainless steel bowl slid noisily across our tile floor. I put no-slip suction cup shower stickers on the bottom of her bowl, and not only does she finish up now, but the bowls also stay in one spot and so are nice and quiet. (A placemat underneath the sliding bowl could also work.)

Bowl location is equally important. Bowls set up in noisy high-traffic areas can be stressful for dogs that aren't typical chowhounds. Your dog's food bowls should be located in a spot that's out of the way, but not so removed that he's completely alone as he eats (for example, outside on the porch or in the garage). Experiment with the placement of your picky dog's bowls. Is he more likely to eat if the bowl is near an interior doorway instead of all the way in the room? (Olive doesn't care that her bowl is all the way inside a room off of our kitchen, but Millie prefers to have her bowl right by the doorway of that room.) Does he seem comfortable having to go completely under the kitchen desk to eat? Is the bowl near the sliding-glass door too distracting for him? Sometimes a simple bowl reset is enough to help a finicky eater find comfort.

Your Presence Is Required

Some picky eaters manipulate their people not only with what they eat, but also *how* they eat. These pups will chow down only if their people are right beside them, which can be a big inconvenience in busy households. Helping your dog learn to eat solo is easier than you think.

Begin the process by standing where you normally do while your dog eats. Don't interact with your dog or pet him to encourage him to eat. During the course of the meal, take a step away from your dog. Don't make a big deal about moving; simply step back quietly. Your dog may stop eating if he notices that you've moved, but don't say anything or even acknowledge your dog. Stay in that position until your dog finishes, and don't make a fuss when your dog is done.

Take two steps away during your dog's next meal. Remain in that new spot until your dog has finished, once again staying neutral. Repeat this process at each meal a step at a time until your dog is able to eat his full meal without needing you right next to him. Keep in mind that you might have to "crab walk" away to the left or right of your dog as he eats instead of backing away, which might put you completely out of his line of vision too quickly.

Predictable Mealtimes

Phyllis left Sam's food out for the entire day so he could grab a few bites if the mood struck. There was no great push for him to finish his meal at breakfast or dinner because he knew it was available to him at all times. Essentially, the food in his bowl was old news, but there was always a savory treat of bite from Phyllis's plate around.

This type of free feeding is problematic for many reasons, and not just for picky eaters. When a dog has his food available all day there's no way to tell if the dog is unwell and not eating the food because there's no clear pattern of the dog actually digging in and finishing the meal. Free feeding can also make bathroom habits less predictable; if you don't know when the food goes in, you probably won't know when it has to come out. Encouraging a dog to eat and actually enjoy his dog food at the appropriate mealtimes can help alleviate some of those issues.

You can help your picky dog understand that mealtime is finite by sticking to a time frame for him to finish the food in his bowl. Put his food down and give him twenty minutes to eat it. If he doesn't finish, pick up the bowl and wait for the next mealtime. (I recommend feeding dogs twice a day.) Assuming that you've made the appropriate changes to the amount of treats and people food that your dog is getting, the type of dog food you're using, the bowl, and the feeding location, it's a safe assumption that your dog will soon understand that mealtimes are for eating and will finish his meal when you put his bowl down.

Take Your Time

Finicky eaters can transform with the right combination of changes to both their diet and the way they consume it. Optimum health is directly related to a complete and balanced diet, so finding a way to reach the picky eater is critical. It might take time, but it's worth the effort, and your happy healthy dog will thank you for it.

thirteen

BARKING

Canine communication takes many forms, but few of them have the potential to be more annoying than unchecked barking. It's perfectly normal for dogs to express themselves through barking, although when it becomes extreme it can cause problems both within your home and around the neighborhood.

Case Study: Chris's dog, Hingle, had always been vocal. The petite Sheltie mix considered it his job to scan the horizon for interlopers and alert the troops with a series of incredibly loud yaps. It wasn't a problem when the pair lived on Chris's parents' remote property, but after Chris moved to a small rental house in a residential neighborhood, Hingle's barking became an issue.

Hingle spent most of his time in the small yard, running along the chain-link fence line and barking any time someone walked by. The barking only stopped when the person or dog disappeared from view. Chris's new neighbors initially made jokes about Hingle's barking, but friendly smiles disappeared when Hingle started his patrols at 7 A.M. on Saturday mornings. Not wanting to make enemies, Chris tried keeping Hingle in the house more often. The clever dog took his job as property protector seriously, and spent his time inside running from window to window, barking out a warning. The amplified noise drove Chris crazy, and he responded by yelling at Hingle. "Knock it off! No bark! *SHUT UP, HINGLE!*" Even worse, the pitch of Hingle's bark was so shrill that he could still be heard outside. Chris knew that things were going to get messy when his next-door neighbors came home with their newborn baby. The proximity of their houses and the intensity of Hingle's barking were a volatile mix.

Possible Outcome One: Chris tries in vain to curb Hingle's barking by yelling at him and using "calm assertive energy," but nothing works. He knows his dog needs exercise and loves being outside, so he is hesitant to deny Hingle yard time. After all, the dog needs to go to the bathroom, and Chris can't help it if Hingle happens to bark when he's doing it! Over time Hingle's barking morphs from being directed at passersby to generalized nonstop barking for the duration of his time outside. Chris's neighbors leave notes for him, asking him to do something about the barking, and each time he promises to try, but the situation doesn't change. He adores Hingle and can't imagine giving him up, so he ignores the problem. But Chris knows that things have gotten out of control when his next-door neighbor with the newborn tells him that he's taking Chris to small-claims court with the support of their other neighbors. Under local statutes Hingle's barking is considered a textbook nuisance case, and with the joint evidence from his neighbors, Chris loses the case and is forced to pay his neighbors $5,000, the maximum fine.

Possible Outcome Two: Chris feels powerless about Hingle's barking. He knows that his neighbors hate him because of it. He knows that Hingle is going slightly insane because Chris doesn't allow him to spend as much time outside in the yard. And he knows that things used to be very different when Hingle lived on his parents' large property. Chris searches online for tips for dealing with a barking dog but finds that shaking a can of pennies at Hingle, for instance, does little to interrupt his passionate barking. With a heavy heart Chris decides that suburban life isn't a fit for his beloved dog, so he packs up Hingle's bed and toys and drives him back to his parents' house. He knows that he'll still be able to see Hingle whenever he wants, but he still tears up as he drives away, feeling like he failed his dog.

Dogs bark for a number of reasons, and determining the drive behind the bark is the first step to dealing with it. There's no single easy fix for barking as the solution depends on the cause. In Hingle's case it was a mix of boredom and territorial barking, a troublesome combination in a small, close-knit community. What could Chris have done to reduce Hingle's barking and make him a happier dog?

What's in a Bark?

Much like every other behavior in the canine repertoire, dogs bark because it works for them, whether it's to scare off a perceived trespasser, signal distress, or self-soothe. Properly dealing with your dog's barking requires that you take a step back and understand the drive behind it. A frustration bark is different from an alarm bark, and so are the ways of tackling them. That said, there is crossover in some of the reasons behind barking. One dog's frustration bark is another dog's frustration/attention-seeking bark. Let's take a closer look at the different types of barks.

Territorial: This type of barking is in response to someone or something coming close to an area that a dog considers his own. Of course this includes your house and yard, and often areas that your dog has "claimed" through frequent visits. There are several dogs in my neighborhood that consider my store theirs (often these are dogs that have been coming to the store since puppyhood), and they bark menacingly at any other dog that dares to come in while they're visiting.

Attention-seeking/demand: Simone and Walker in Chapter 11 demonstrated the challenges of attention-seeking barking. A dog that barks in the hopes of getting something, whether it's your focus, food, play, or access to the outdoors, is engaging in attention-seeking barking.

Alarm: Alarm barkers go off at the slightest provocation. The sound of a dropped pot in the kitchen or a noisy truck on the street are enough to incite an alarm barker. Alarm barking can come on so suddenly that it even seems to startle the dog that's doing it.

Boredom: Understimulated dogs can resort to boredom barking as a means to entertain and self-soothe. Boredom barks are usually repetitive and have a similar pitch. A friend once described to me the very specific barks of a neighborhood dog left in the yard alone the entire day: "It was 'Aroo-roo-roo. Ruff. Ruff. Aroo-roo-roo. Ruff. Ruff. Aroo-roo-roo. Ruff. Ruff.' *All* day long!" It was clear by the predictable pattern that the dog wasn't barking at anything that she heard or saw, she was making noise for the sake of making noise.

Fear: Dogs that bark out of fear are often misunderstood. The barking might appear menacing, but it's usually indicative of a dog in conflict. Clients will tell me that their dog barks at people of different races or tall men in hats because their dog "doesn't like" them, when the dog might actually be afraid of them (often due to a lack of socialization to the people in question) and is barking to attempt to increase their distance from the person.

Excitement: "Talkative" dogs usually engage in excitement barking when they're getting ready to do something fun. Going for a walk, daily meal prep, or taking a ride in the car triggers a cacophony of joyful noise. It can verge on attention-seeking barking.

Frustration: The dog that chases a squirrel up a tree, or sees a cat on the other side of the fence and can't get to it, or can't reach a ball that's rolled under the couch is likely to engage in frustration barking. There's a barrier between the dog and something it wants, whether it's a fence or a leash (or a couch!), and the dog reacts to his powerlessness with a fit of barking.

Play: Play barkers get so excited by the game that they can't help but give a running commentary. They might bark at other dogs they're having a good time with as if scolding them (the "fun police" of the dog park), or they might bark directly at their playmate as they romp. Herding dogs are pros at this type of barking.

Separation distress: Dogs that are uncomfortable being left home alone might engage in prolonged howly barking. These dogs are intolerant of being alone, whether while their person walks out to get the mail or leaves for work for the day. This type of barking is related to but not the same as true separation anxiety. Distress barking doesn't share the other hallmarks of true separation anxiety like elimination in the house, destruction, and escape attempts at exit points that are so extreme that the dog often self-injures.

Management Solutions for Barking

Dog challenges can be dealt with in two ways: using training to bring about a behavioral change or implementing a management solution that sidesteps the problem. For example, if your dog barks at the pizza delivery person you can train your dog to go to his bed and wait quietly instead of crowding the front door, or you can manage the situation by putting him in a different room while you receive the delivery. Management solutions are obviously easier to implement and can bring about dramatic change with minimal effort. The following are some straightforward management options for some of the barkers listed.

Lower the window film an inch at a time until you can remove it completely.

Block the view: helpful for alarm barkers and territorial barkers

Putting up a visual barrier between the barker and the barkee can decrease a dog's drive to bark. An open chain-link fence that gives the dog a full view of the horizon can be transformed quickly and affordably with plastic privacy weave, available at most large hardware stores. That said, many barkers are equally stimulated by sound. We removed a chain-link fence and put up a five-foot privacy fence in the backyard at my former house, and even though my Boston Terrier and Boxer were no longer able to see the dog in the yard behind us, they could hear the noise from her collar when she came close to the property line. The fence was a wonderful addition that dramatically cut down on the drama since the dogs were no longer nose-to-nose through the chain link, but we still had occasional barky episodes. (Stay tuned for how I dealt with those!)

Common advice for territorial and alarm barkers that sound off while *inside* the house is to close drapes or blinds so the dog can't see outside. While it's a decent management solution, it's not necessarily pleasant to live in a dark house. Privacy window films—the opaque peel and stick covering available at most hardware stores—are a great alternative because they block your dog's view but still let light in. Even better, you don't have to keep the film up forever. Simply install it a few inches above your dog's sightline (you don't have to cover the entire window) and gradually lower the film an inch at a time over the course of several weeks. There's a good chance that combining blocked visual access with some simple training cues will make your dog less likely to engage in intense territorial barking.

Less solo yard time: helpful for territorial barkers, alarm barkers, and boredom barkers

If your dog spends his time in the yard barking, whether it's at perceived trespassers or because he's bored and lonely, it makes sense to decrease your dog's amount of solo yard time. The barking is working for your dog on some level, meaning in his mind he's scaring the trespasser away ("When I bark, that guy in the brown uniform leaves. Great strategy!"), or he's soothing himself while on his own. While the bored yard barker might drive the neighbors crazy, this is a dog to be pitied. Although people like to believe that dogs enjoy time hanging out in the sunshine, dogs are pack animals that want and need to spend time with their people. Instead of sending your dog to the yard alone, put your shoes on and spend more time with your dog in the great outdoors!

Increase exercise: helpful for all barkers!

Nearly every dog can benefit from more exercise, but particularly barkers. If your dog's mental and physical needs aren't being met you might find yourself dealing with a bored, frustrated, or demanding barker. Check out the suggestions on pages 160–161 for ways to engage your dog's brain and body. Remember, a tired dog is a content dog!

Busy toys: helpful for attention-seeking/ demand barkers, boredom barkers, separation-distress barkers

Hard rubber toys that dispense treats like the ones detailed on pages 45, 48–49, and 161–162 can help redirect many a barker. They're a quick fix for the boredom barker and the attention-seeking barker, like Simone's dog Walker. They're particularly helpful for dogs suffering from separation distress. Rather than leaving the distressed barker alone with no other job but pacing the house and looking out the windows, teaching him to love busy toys can keep him happily occupied as you leave for the day. It helps to create a ritual around stuffing the toy and then handing it over to your dog, so that his anticipation builds as you prepare the goodies. (You can also hide a few extras throughout the house to keep your dog busy longer.) I've worked with many dogs who are so excited to get their paws on the toy that they barely notice when their person walks out the door.

White-noise machine: helpful for alarm barkers and separation-distress barkers

One of my favorite quick fixes for alarm barkers is turning on a white-noise machine, particularly for apartment dwellers who have to deal with the sounds of neighbors right outside their door all day. The machine's steady unchanging sound masks many of the incidental noises that would normally trigger barking. I have in one in my bedroom, and my alarm barker Olive doesn't react to anything when it's turned on. (Even neighbor voices that I can clearly hear!)

Homeopathic and pheromone-based treatments: helpful for fear barkers and distress barkers

While they can't bring about a complete change of behavior the way prescribed anti-anxiety medication can, natural treatments like distilled flower essences and plug-in pheromone diffusers can offer some comfort for nervous barkers.

Training Solutions for Barkers

While the management techniques listed on the previous pages can certainly put a dent in barking challenges, they don't actually change the dog's responses to the triggers. It takes training to bring about behavioral change. As always, remaining mindful during this process will help you find resolution faster. Take a step back and determine if you're accidentally reinforcing your dog's barking. When someone rings the doorbell, do you walk to the door asking your dog, "Who's here? Who's here?" which encourages him to sound off? Do you put down your dog's food bowl when he's barking at you for it? Using the management techniques listed in conjunction with the corresponding training suggestions below is an effective way to handle nearly all of the different types of barkers.

Teach "hush": helpful for territorial barkers and alarm barkers, as well as some excitement and play barkers

Many of us would like to allow our dogs to bark for security reasons (a barking dog is an effective crime deterrent) if only there was a way to turn it off when necessary. Teaching your dog to "hush" when asked is just that: a way to allow your dog to bark for a bit and then stop when you ask.

When you're first teaching "hush," hold the treat in your hand and place it near your dog's nose.

To teach "hush" grab a handful of small tasty treats. When your dog begins barking place a treat in the palm of your hand and walk over to where he's standing. Put your fist with the treat enclosed inside in front of your dog's nose and allow him to sniff at it. Aha! He's no longer barking! Take advantage of this moment of solitude by telling your dog "hush" in a soft voice (you're "naming" the silence), praise your dog, and then drop the treat to the ground. If he goes back to barking, repeat the process, but this time toss the treat a few steps away from where he's standing. (Make sure that he sees you throw it!) This process is cumbersome initially because it requires that you're close to your dog when he's barking, but the eventual goal is that you can tell your dog "hush" from a distance away and he'll understand.

Continue using the food lure in front of your dog's nose for repetitions spread out over a few days. Try several repetitions where you place your closed hand several inches away from your dog's nose instead of directly in front of it. This makes the food lure less obvious, and may help your dog to understand that the food doesn't have to be right in front of him in order for it to be earned.

Next, test your dog's understanding of what he's learning; walk up to your dog when he's barking and just say "hush." You should see him look up at you as if to say, "Where's my treat?!" Keep in mind that you shouldn't have to shout the word or repeat it. (If you do then he's not ready for the verbal cue alone. Go back to the hand prompt for a while.) When your dog

"Thank You"

Some dogs start their barking fits with a few rumbly grumbly noises before they go into a full-tilt meltdown. (Envision when your dog hears something crash outside and lets out a "Woof? Woof?" and then looks at you as if to say, "Do I need to be worried about that noise?") Sometimes all it takes to prevent a barky breakdown is to tell your dog, "Thanks, I've got it!" It's not something that you actually *teach* your dog, it's all about the manner in which you say it. It seems odd, but confidently telling your dog "Got it—thanks!" meaning, "Never fear, I'm handling this catastrophic event that's just outside our front door," is often enough to convince your dog that there's nothing to worry about, and that you're on patrol for the moment. I say it when my dogs hear our neighbor rattling the garbage cans and often get an extra "wuff" or two from them, and then they settle down. It works in many scenarios!

looks to you for the treat, praise him heartily and then toss it a few steps away so that he has to leave his barking post to get it. Then engage your quiet dog in a few sits, downs, or a short game so that he realizes that listening to "hush" makes good things happen! Over time you should be able to say "hush" from a distance and he'll stop barking and come to you to collect (provided he's not barking at something highly distressing right in front of him). Continue rewarding the cessation of barking for a *long* time. You're competing with a self-reinforcing hardwired behavior, so you should pay your dog handsomely for listening to you.

Train a "magic whistle": helpful for territorial barkers, alarm barkers, and some frustration barkers

So how did I deal with my Boston Terrier Zeke and Boxer Sumner's barky preoccupation with our neighbor dog despite the five-foot fence between them? I taught them that when they heard me blow a whistle that they needed to stop barking and come running to me *no matter what.* My "magic whistle" was so effective that they would stop midbark (the dogs were often almost nose-to-nose beneath the fence line) and come running back to me to collect payment! Using a whistle is especially helpful for situations where your dog is barking at a great distance from you, where a verbal cue might not have the same stopping power. The beauty of using a whistle instead of your voice to get your dog to stop barking is that the sound is so distinct and rewarding that most dogs can't help but respond to it. It's a powerful—and yes, almost magical—tool, but can you figure out the secret of the whistle? It's really just a recall in disguise!

The first step is picking the right whistle for you. "Silent" dog whistles have a coolness factor, but most of them aren't truly silent. They're quieter than most whistles, but the sound is still audible to humans. You can also opt for a very loud traditional referee-style whistle. The type you pick doesn't matter, it's what you do with it that will make all the difference.

The training process is simple. Bring your dog to a distraction-free part of your house and blow the whistle once when your dog is standing close to you. Don't do it in such a way that it startles your dog—blow the whistle softly for the first few repetitions. Immediately give your dog a special treat. Repeat this step a few times in different parts of your house, making sure that your dog is readily coming up to you each time you blow the whistle. Your dog should move toward you quickly and look excited every time he hears it.

After your dog is reliably approaching you each time you blow the whistle, try a few surprise practice sessions. Blow the whistle while in a different room from your dog when he doesn't expect it, and reward him

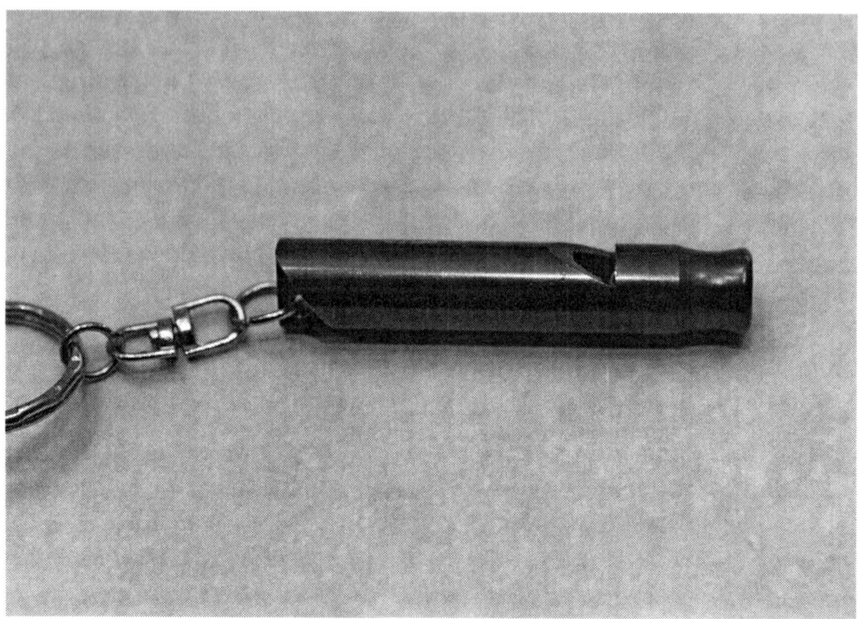

A "magic whistle" can work wonders for yard barkers.

with a treat when he runs up to you. Make this step a game—have fun with your dog! Try introducing a few low-level distractions, like blowing the whistle while your dog is "helping" someone loading the dishwasher, or while someone is browsing through your dog's toy basket as if to find the perfect toy to play with. (The level of distractibility varies by dog, so choose your distraction wisely. Using the toy basket might be too much for a toy-driven dog. Don't set your dog up to fail!)

By now your dog should understand that the whistle predicts treats and lots of praise, so make the process a little tougher by taking it outside. (If your dog is still iffy with his responses, keep practicing inside in low-distraction areas until you're getting predictable joyful responses.) Let your dog meander around your yard and then blow the whistle when he's just out of sight. As always, treat and praise. Continue doing practice drills inside and outside the house, cementing the idea that the whistle brings wonderful goodies.

The first time you use the whistle in a real-life barking scenario can be nerve-wracking, but your practice will have paid off. If possible, toot the whistle *before* your dog surrenders to the barking fit, when he's just starting to respond to whatever has triggered him. Praise him as he makes his way over to you, and as always, reward him for his efforts. Success! Short-circuiting barking is a big deal, so continue to reward your dog with food for longer than you would think necessary. I *still* reward Millie and Olive for listening to the whistle after several years. Their responses are so

The Magic Whistle Drawback

Although the whistle can be an amazing tool for dealing with barking, there's a problem with relying too heavily on a piece of equipment: it can't help you if you don't have it in your hand. I've had quite a few instances when my dogs were barking at something on the horizon at 6:00 in the morning and the whistle was nowhere to be found. Luckily my dogs have generalized their "barking recall" to the sound of any whistle, so I can whistle with my mouth and they still come running. If you're concerned about this type of occasional equipment failure, you can pair the sound of your trained whistle with either a whistle sound you make with your mouth or a loud hand clap. Simply add the new "equipment-failure" sound *before* you blow the whistle for several practice repetitions. The new sound becomes the predictor for the magic whistle, thereby ensuring that you have a backup when you need it. Can you just rely on the equipment failure sound for all of your magic whistle needs? Of course, if you give it the same kid-glove handling as you do the magic whistle, meaning you always reward your dog after you use it, you don't use it casually and your dog responds to it readily. That said, I adore my magic whistle, and so do my dogs!

lightning fast and impressive (they always come running from the other end of our one-acre yard, even when they're barking at deer on the other side of the fence) that they deserve to get a morsel every time.

Ignore barking: helpful for attention-seeking barking, play barking, and frustration barking

Ignoring your barking dog is a possible solution for any type of barking, of course, but it's not a great fit for dogs that are barking out of fear or distress, as these dogs are in crisis and need to be helped. Ignoring a dog that's barking for your attention is another story. As illustrated with Simone and Walker, attention-seeking barking thrives on our focus. It can be accidentally rewarded and strengthened in ways that aren't obvious to us, so that even something as seemingly benign as a glance in the dog's direction when he's demand barking is enough to encourage him to keep at it. As described in Chapter 11, *actively* ignoring the attention-seeking barking is a way to take the power out of the behavior. If the bark doesn't summon you to feed faster, walk sooner, or play longer, eventually it will go away. If I haven't said it enough yet, I'll repeat it: dogs do what works.

The same goes for the frustration barker. Rescuing the ball from beneath the couch or opening the door to let him chase the squirrel in the yard when the barker “asks” reinforces the idea that barking is a viable strategy. Ignoring the frustration barker helps him to understand that noisy dogs get nothing.

When it comes to play barking you can also opt to ignore the barking by chalking it up to normal dog behavior. This isn’t “actively” ignoring the barking, which you would do with attention-seeking barking, it’s “opting-out” ignoring. Frolicking dogs bark, so if your neighbors don’t mind and you don’t mind, you can certainly let the commentary continue as your dog plays.

Institute an interrupt: helpful for attention-seeking barking, play barking, and excitement barking

Sometimes ignoring a barker isn’t enough. If your dog is barking at you because he’s excited that you’re getting ready to leash him up for a walk, ignoring him might not drive the message home quickly enough. (“Why isn’t my person clipping the leash on me? I see it in her hand and we’re clearly about to go for a walk, so I’ll just keep barking until it’s time!”) In situations like this you can help your dog understand that not only does barking not work; it actually makes his goal less likely.

An interrupt is an efficient way of short circuiting a determined barker by stopping doing whatever the dog is barking about. For example, instead of accidentally reinforcing the barking by putting on the leash and commencing with the walk, drop the leash and walk away instead. If your timing is good—meaning you drop the leash the moment your dog begins to bark—this dramatic playacting will have an impact. The interrupt applies in many barking scenarios. If your little dog barks at you when he wants to join you on the couch, stand up and leave the room. If your dog barks at you the entire time you’re prepping his dinner, put down the bowl and do something else until he’s quiet. If your dog barks at you when he wants you to throw the ball, let it fall from your hand and walk away. It’s almost as if the sound of your dog’s voice makes you do the opposite of what he wants.

Once your dog is quiet you can go back to doing what you were doing prior to the barking. If seeing you back near his bowl or with the leash in your hand revs him up again, repeat the interrupt. You’ll probably have to repeat it several consecutive times (and in several ongoing sessions) before your dog understands the correlation between his behavior and the consequence.

Your timing should be good on both sides of the behavior, meaning you should institute the interrupt immediately when your dog begins barking, and in the *initial* stages of the process, recommence what you were doing just as quickly when your dog manages to quiet down. When you begin helping your dog understand the interrupt process, be quick to acknowledge his quietness. It won't be easy for him to maintain silence during the beginning stages—he's used to barking to get what he wants—so make it easy for him to "win" by acknowledging even a few seconds of quiet. Once he starts to understand that quiet works and not barking, you can require him to hold the silence a little longer before you go back to what you were doing. Some clever dogs make an association that the new acceptable behavior is "Bark-bark-then-quiet" instead of silence alone. Gradually extend the amount of time that your dog needs to be quiet before you recommence, so that he understands that silence is the best strategy of all.

Diffuse departures: helpful for separation-distress barkers

Being left alone can be an anxiety-ridden process for some dogs. Our very predictable predeparture rituals signal our intent long before we have to walk out the door, which can roil a departure-sensitive dog as you get closer and closer to leaving. Often something as simple as changing up your routine can help to soothe an anxious barker before he even begins.

Instead of engaging in the same patterns before you leave, try making your rituals less predictable. If you typically eat breakfast, then shower, then walk your dog, reverse the order. Or implement a new step in the middle of your departure routine, like sitting down to watch a few minutes of the morning news, or read the paper at the counter for a bit. The idea is that instead of building up to leaving in the same predictable pattern so that your dog follows your progress with stress-filled anticipation ("This happens, then this happens, then this, then he *leaves!* It's awful!"), your exact departure time remains a mystery. Check your drama level when you leave as well. Don't act as if you'll never see your dog again! Be matter-of-fact and unemotional when it comes time to go. A simple "good-bye" and chin scratch is more than enough to convey your adoration without unduly dramatizing your farewell.

Even better, engage in some play with your dog before you leave for the day. Get his brain and body working with a game of find the toy, or practice some quick trick training. You can transition from interacting with your dog to giving him an activity toy that will keep him happy, and then quietly take your leave. Although this step alone won't cure a distress barker, making your departures less predictable and stressful along with adding some of the following management suggestions can help to bring an anxious dog some peace.

A Word about Bark-Control Collars

There are many different types of antibark collars on the market, from those that emit a high-pitched sound or a spray of citronella when the dog makes a noise to those that shock your dog every time he barks. Bark collars seem like an immediate and simple fix for a barking problem, but there are cautions to consider before trying one.

- Does the collar use pain to train? A collar that promises a "correction" because of "stimulation" is actually using a painful shock to stop the barking. In this enlightened age of dog training, there is no need to train with pain.
- Have you considered why your dog is barking? It's not fair to slap a bark-control collar on a dog that's suffering from anxiety or fear-based barking. It could actually make the problem worse.
- Have you tried to address your dog's barking through positive training? Before you resort to a punitive method to address barking, ask yourself if you've really exhausted all of your training options.

Desensitization and counterconditioning: helpful for fear barkers and distress barkers

Dogs that bark out of fear require controlled rehabilitation. Although some of the previous suggestions can chip away at fear barking, true behavioral change requires choreographed training. The process, detailed in Chapter 11, is involved and requires that you become a student of your dog's emotional states. It takes time and dedication to work through any fear-based behavioral problem, but the outcome is a happier, better-adjusted dog.

Reward the absence of barking: helpful for all barkers

The normally barky dog that opts to be quiet in the face of temptations deserves to be lavished with attention. Many dogs are used to acknowledgment only when they're being naughty and loud, so taking the time to pet and praise a quiet dog is a paradigm shift. *Any* time your dog decides to be quiet instead of barking is worthy of acknowledgment. Did your dog spot a neighbor outside your window and turn to you instead of freaking out? Praise him! Give him a treat! Did he let you help your child with her homework without offering editorial comment the entire time? Have a love-fest! Did he bark once and then pace in front of the couch that ate his tennis ball instead of chanting at it? Give that dog a round of fetch on the house!

I've dealt with several types of barking with Olive, and it's been incredibly rewarding to watch her figuring out what works in our household. Her alarm, territorial, attention-seeking, frustration, play, and excitement barking (yes, we have our hands full with Olive!) have all abated to very manageable levels. Although barking will always be a part of her repertoire, she knows how far she can take it, and we know the greatness that she's capable of.

Barking is one of the most universally frustrating canine behaviors, but it doesn't have to be a deal breaker as it was for Craig and Hingle. Identifying the trigger and then chipping away at it through management and training will bring about a harmonious home and happy neighbors!

fourteen

DIGGING

Like barking, digging can serve many purposes for a dog. Digging holes is a way to stave off boredom because it's fun and there's clear progress as the dog gets closer to its goal. Sometimes you can almost see the digging dog estimating the hole size and shape like a builder doing a renovation! Occasionally the digger looking for entertainment unearths something that plays back, like roots or insects. Some diggers want to protect their bones or toys, so they bury them throughout the yard. (Many digger dogs think that the couch or their dog bed can suffice as a hiding spot, although the camouflage provided by these areas is minimal!) Dogs like terriers are driven to dig by instinct to unearth prey. Northern breeds with thick coats might dig on a summer day to find cool earth beneath the surface. Sadly, some dogs dig to escape their confinement, seeking greener pastures beyond the fence line. And some dogs dig just because it's fun!

Because digging is highly reinforcing in so many different ways, the problem rarely goes away on its own. Dealing with a pock-marked yard (or scratched-raw couch) requires intervention and creativity.

Case Study: Carter and Alyssa added Ted the Lab mix to their family after many years of promising their two kids a dog. The family was overjoyed to welcome the high-energy adolescent, and they tried to make sure their new rescue dog adjusted to their lifestyle. They enrolled Ted in obedience classes, but because of their busy schedules they could only attend two sessions. Ted learned an iffy "sit" and that was about it. He was wild and unpredictable.

They tried to walk Ted to tire him out (or to be more accurate, get dragged down the street by him), but it seemed that his energy levels never dipped below manic activity. Rather than let him tear around the house they opted to put him in their sprawling fenced yard for several hours every day in the hopes that he'd play himself into a calmer state. It never worked, but Carter and Alyssa appreciated the quiet in the house while Ted was outside.

After a rainy week Alyssa noticed that every time she let Ted in the house his paws and muzzle were muddy. She could understand dirty paws, but she wasn't sure why his face was dirty too, so she quietly followed him the next time she let him out. She hadn't actually been out to the yard in weeks because of the inclement weather, so she was shocked to discover a vast excavation in and around her landscaped flower beds. As she surveyed the damage, Ted planted his nose in the turned-up earth, breathed in, and began digging as if he could smell buried treasure.

Possible Outcome One: Unwilling to keep rambunctious Ted inside during the day, Carter and Alyssa continued to let him rule the yard and dig to his heart's content. They hated his digging, but the tradeoff of keeping "Hurricane Ted" inside wasn't an option. As winter turned to spring, the results of his hole habit became even more apparent. Not only did the yard look terrible, but many of the trees, shrubs, and flowers withered away instead of coming back to life. Carter and Alyssa had spent years working on their yard only to have it trashed by Ted within months.

Possible Outcome Two: Ted enjoyed his time in the yard but often wanted to come inside after an hour of being on his own. Alyssa didn't want to have to deal with Ted as she worked on the computer or prepped dinner, so she left him outside. Over time his digging habit became more focused near the edge of the fence line, where he could hear people and other dogs passing by. He managed to find a soft patch of dirt near the doorway that easily gave way. Because his family rarely came out to check on him, Ted worked at the hole over the course of days like a prisoner digging an escape route, until it was big enough for him to slip through. Ted took off late one afternoon, and his people didn't realize he was missing until he showed up at their front door hours later, barking and scratching to get back in.

Digging problems can range from a mild aesthetic nuisance to a full-blown lifestyle problem for dogs that dig to escape. Dealing with digging requires a mindful look at the reasons driving the behavior. Let's explore what makes a digger tick.

Solutions for Bored Diggers

One of the most common reasons a dog digs is because he's bored. Much like Ted's reaction to his yard confinement in outcome one, a dog on his own outside will resort to finding his own entertainment, whether it's barking at the noises he hears in the distance, harassing passersby, or digging. Of course the obvious solution for a bored digger like Ted is to decrease the amount of time alone time in the yard, and increase the amount of stimulation he's getting from you.

Although it might seem that a dog would prefer to hang out in the great outdoors on a beautiful day, most dogs would rather be with their people. (Of course, there are exceptions, like senior dogs that appreciate dozing in the sun.) Unfortunately, the trend I've noticed with dogs that resort to

Dogs dig for many reasons. Determining the reason your dog is digging will help you stop it, or redirect it.

boredom digging in the yard is that their people don't seem to have enough time for them, whether to teach them how to be a gentleman indoors or appropriately exercise them to wear them out. If Ted's people had pursued his training and helped him understand how to act inside their house, they wouldn't have been "forced" to put him outside for such long periods of time, which in turn created his digging habit. So what can be done to help a bored digger?

- **Increase stimulation:** Take the time to really connect with your dog at least once a day, above and beyond your usual walks. Play games that engage his body, like fetch and tug, as well as games that get his brain working too, like find the toy (page 53). Do trick training, where you work on skills that are fun for fun's sake. Focus on wearing out your dog first and then give him yard time if you must and if he so desires. He'll be more likely to relax outside instead of resorting to digging if he's been exercised beforehand.
- **Give your dog something to do:** If you feel that your dog must spend time outside unsupervised, provide him with something constructive to do while he's out there. Give him engaging hard rubber treat-dispensing toys, or consider giving him bones that are too messy to eat indoors, like raw marrow bones. The goal is to keep your dog happy with something sanctioned rather than forcing him to resort to digging to fill the time.

- **Don't leave your dog alone in the yard for long periods:** This is the most basic "fix" for boredom diggers. You can easily manage the problem by not giving your dog the opportunity to engage in the behavior. Allow him time outside, but keep him occupied and happy in the house as well.

Solutions for Hide-Away Diggers

Dogs that want to hide their treasures can be driven to dig almost anywhere, from the yard to your carpet and furniture. After the excavation, whether actual in the yard or imagined inside the house, the goody is carefully covered either with gentle paws or by nosing the dirt back into place. It's not only a potentially destructive behavior; it can also get expensive if your dog hides the toys and bones you buy for him. So how can we help a hide-away digger?

- **Provide a dig pit:** Rather than trying to squelch this hardwired "survival" behavior, it helps to direct it to an acceptable spot in the yard that you select. Pick a spot that works for you from an aesthetic standpoint and will also work for your dog, one that mimics the spots he's chosen on his own. It's likely that he's selecting out-of-the-way areas

Rather than letting your dog dig up your flower beds, redirect his digging to a sanctioned digging spot that you create for him.

under trees or shrubs for his treasures, so don't pick a dig pit spot in a wide-open area.

Make the borders of the dig pit obvious to your dog, either by ringing it with bricks or stones, or if you're handy, building low retaining walls. The size depends on your dog's size and digging style. You'll want to give your dog enough room to dig a bunch of holes, so that he feels that he has options for his treasures. Fill the pit with soft loose dirt or sand, so that it gives easily under your dog's paws and feels more luxurious than the dense compacted dirt in your yard. (I prefer sand since it's cleaner, but some dogs are initially spooked by sand's unique texture. It took Millie an uncomfortable hour before she finally started enjoying digging her paws in the sand at the beach, but now she loves it!)

When your pit is complete, bury a few surprises like novel treats and a new toy just below the surface. Help your dog find these goodies, and praise him as he familiarizes himself with his new playground. Continue to hide surprises in the dig pit so that your dog starts to understand that this magical spot not only safely hides the goodies he wants to keep for later, but also offers up something wonderful every time he digs!

I like to "name" digging behavior by telling the dog what he's doing as he's doing it, so when the dog begins to dig I'll say, "digdigdigdigdig!" and praise him for doing so. (The word actually sounds like the behavior, so I can't help but smile as I chant it!) This helps if your dog slips up and opts to dig somewhere other than his dig pit. Interrupt him by saying "eh-eh!" or any other sharp noise that will get him to stop, and then lead him over to his dig pit and tell him, "digdigdig!"

- **Provide an indoor dig pit:** If your dog likes to bury things both inside the house and outside, give him a sanctioned spot somewhere inside your house as well. Cut down a large cardboard box so that the sides are low enough for your dog to step into, or if you want a more permanent solution, invest in a long low plastic storage container. (Chain hardware stores have every size you can imagine.) Cut up a stack of old T-shirts into long strips of fabric and put the fabric strips into the digging box. Find an out-of-the-way spot for the box and go through the same introductory steps as with the outside dig pit. You can experiment with the box filler if you're confident that your dog won't ingest it, like ripped-up pieces of foam. The goal is to use something that's soft and easy for you to pick up.
- **Don't give your dog high-value items to take outside:** My dog-training mantra applies here as well: if it's predictable, it's

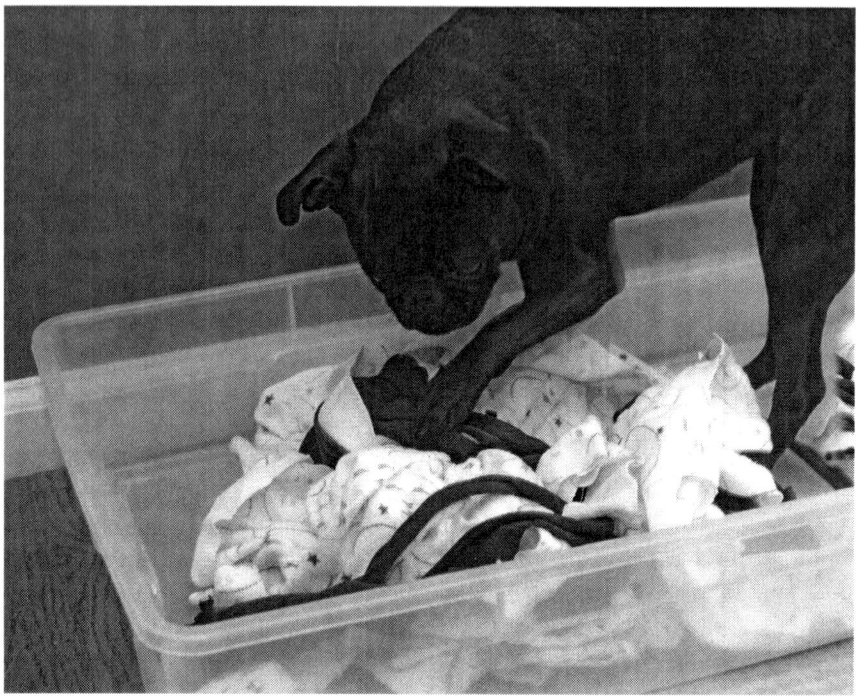

An indoor dig pit filled with strips of old fabric is a great way to redirect dogs that bury their bones in the couch.

preventable. If you don't have a dig pit and *know* that your dog buries every expensive bully stick you give to him, never to be seen (or chewed) again, don't give him the opportunity to do so. I have a beloved customer at my store who comes in twice a month to buy more $8 bones because his dog buries them in the yard every chance he gets. While the merchant in me loves his frequent visits, the trainer in me wonders why his dog keeps having the opportunity to "lose" the expensive bones. (Of course, there's a good chance that my customer has enough disposable income to buy as many bones as he wants!) To avoid this expensive habit, give the hide-away digger bones only inside the house, or if you want to indulge his habit, let him take the bone or chew outside once it's long past its "sell-by" date.

Solutions for the Prey-Driven Digger

Some dogs are hardwired to "go to ground" in search of animals below the surface. Not only is digging fun for these dogs, it also has the potential to be highly rewarding if they're ever successful in unearthing something. (Even the scent of long-departed prey provides a thrill.) Dogs digging after animals underground will become fixated on specific spots, particularly at that animal's entry and exit points, or the telltale mounds of dirt these subterranean dwellers kick up as they move through the yard.

Prey diggers aren't just doing so because it's fun, they're doing it because they have an undeniable drive to do so. Terriers and Dachshunds are famous for their tenacious need to unearth small animals. Redirecting these single-minded dogs is difficult, so while offering a solution like a dig pit might seem like a decent option, unless you're also burying live creatures for your dog to unearth, it just won't have the same appeal as the rest of your yard. So what can be done about prey-driven diggers?

- **Remove temptation:** Encourage the beasts your dog is after to move on to a different yard by using natural repellents, like flooding the animal's tunnel with a mix of equal parts of castor oil dishwashing soap and cayenne pepper, using yard-safe grub control (moles eat grubs), or placing vibrating wind spinners at various points throughout the animal's tunnel. Keep in mind that commercial pest removal services that use chemicals are dangerous for the vermin *and* for your dog.
- **Make creature areas inaccessible:** If you know that there is a specific area in your yard where vermin have taken up residence, consider installing a temporary fencing system to keep your dog from reaching it.
- **Supervise your dog in the yard:** This solution fits for nearly all of the digging issues. By accompanying your dog into the yard, you're able to interrupt the digging behavior as it begins and redirect your dog to an acceptable activity, like fetch or tug.
- **Indulge your dog's drive in other spaces:** Take your dog on walks in the woods on a long leash (over eight feet) and encourage the digging behavior in a space that can take the abuse. Help your dog find creature holes and tell him "digidigdig" as he merrily complies.

Solutions for Digging Dogs Seeking Temperature Control

Conventional advice for people whose dogs are digging to cool down or warm up include providing the dog with swimming pools, fans, cooling or heating pads, doghouses, shade shelters, beds, or blankets. I say rubbish to all of it. If the weather is so extreme that your dog is resorting to digging as a means to find comfort, *bring your dog inside.* Granted, some dogs enjoy the heat, so providing a sanctioned dig pit to cool off in is a fine option, but if you're jumping through hoops to keep your dog cool or warm outside, do him a favor and bring him into a climate-controlled environment.

Solutions for Escape Diggers

Similarly, typical advice for people whose dogs tunnel out of the yard is to fortify the base of the fence line with chicken wire, cement, and boulders. Although that's fine advice from a safety perspective, it doesn't get to the heart of the issue. Instead of turning your yard into Fort Knox, I suggest mindfulness and taking a step back. *Why* does your dog want to escape confinement? Is he an intact male on the hunt for females? Neuter him for health and safety reasons. Is he left alone in the yard for too long and is desperate for interaction, like Ted in Possible Outcome Two? Address his boredom by increasing your interactions with him and decreasing his yard time. Is he frightened by something in the yard? Work on desensitizing him to the yard by following the program in Chapter 6. Instead of putting a bandage on the wound by shoring up your fencing, work on addressing the core issue first.

CONCLUSION: IT TAKES TIME

As I finished this book, it was winter, complete with weeks of snow and mud. There were days when I felt like all I did was wipe eight dirty paws over and over and over again. And now, each time I bend down and grasp Olive's front paw in my hand, I'm reminded of our early paw-cleaning interactions and how far we've come since her surprising reaction as a puppy. That growl that shocked me at ten weeks old is now just a memory. When I let Millie and Olive in from the yard I say, "Go to your spot!" and they happily wait on the small throw rug that I use as their home base. Millie has always been tolerant of my wipe-downs, so I usually take care of her paws first, using her good behavior as a primer for what Olive should do as well. Then I move on to Olive, who offers up a paw for me as if to say, "I got this, Ma!" I still make a big deal about successful paw-wiping episodes even though she's been great for ages now. I frequently give them each a little treat for being so good about it, and I still thank my lucky stars that I took the time to address Olive's handling sensitivities before they got out of control. We had off-days as we worked through those issues, like when I discovered during her bath that her sensitivities extended down to her tail. It took time and patience to get her through her various challenges, but the outcome—her calm acceptance of my full-body ministrations—still makes me proud.

I recently watched a TV interview about an assistance dog-training school, and the director of the school lauded the dogs in his program—and dogs in general—for their temperament, saying "Dogs *never* have a bad day. They're always happy!" But dogs *do* have off-days and they *do* have emotions other than happiness. It does them a grave disservice to believe otherwise. There are nuances to our dogs' emotions that most certainly can have an impact on any behavioral problem-solving you attempt. Think about the time your dog moped around the house when a beloved family member was away on a trip, or how he went on a three-day hunger strike when you adopted a new puppy. Always remember that your dog isn't a computer waiting to be programmed. (If only it were that easy!)

Olive and Millie say, "Go ahead and wipe our paws—we can take it!"

There's an ebb and flow to training, particularly when it comes to problem solving. It's likely you'll have amazing successes and surprising lows as you go through the process, but remember—it's a process. You're not training in a laboratory, where every aspect can be carefully orchestrated for maximum results. The real world is messy! You might have a week of near-perfect potty training only to have a surprise slip-up on a busy Saturday. Or you might have redirected your dog's jumpy greeting behavior to a few manageable hops when your neighbor stops by and encourages your dog to leap up and hug him.

Yes, it's a huge bummer when your training plan momentarily derails, but life happens. Setbacks happen. There is no "As-seen-on-TV" solution or magic wand that you can use to immediately and safely change your dog's behavior (although there is a magic whistle!). As long as you remain mindful, tune into what your dog is telling you, and stay the course with positive dog-friendly training, you will get the results you're seeking, and your relationship with your dog *will* continue to blossom and grow.

INDEX

CPSIA information can be obtained at www.ICGtesting.com
Printed in the USA
BVOW05s0843130614

356316BV00002B/2/P